ISBN 978-0-428-98912-5
PIBN 10810317

TRANSFORMATION:

OR, THE

ROMANCE OF MONTE BENI.

BY

NATHANIEL HAWTHORNE,

AUTHOR OF "THE SCARLET LETTER," ETC. ETC.

IN THREE VOLUMES.

VOL. II.

LONDON:

SMITH, ELDER & CO., 65, CORNHILL.

M.DCCC.LX.

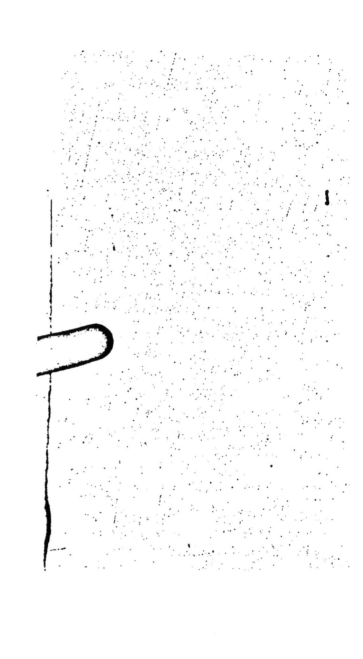

TRANSFORMATION:

OR, THE

ROMANCE OF MONTE BENI.

BY

NATHANIEL HAWTHORNE,

AUTHOR OF "THE SCARLET LETTER," ETC. ETC.

IN THREE VOLUMES.

VOL. II.

LONDON:
SMITH, ELDER & CO., 65, CORNHILL.
M.DCCC.LX.

CONTENTS

OF THE SECOND VOLUME.

————◇◇————

ROMANCE OF MONTE BENI.

CHAPTER I.

MIRIAM'S TROUBLE.

As usual of a moonlight evening, several carriages stood at the entrance of this famous ruin, and the precincts and interior were anything but a solitude. The French sentinel on duty beneath the principal archway eyed our party curiously, but offered no obstacle to their admission. Within, the moonlight filled and flooded the great empty space; it glowed upon tier above tier of ruined, grass-grown arches, and made them even too distinctly visible. The splendour of the revela-

tion took away that inestimable effect of dim-
ness and mystery by which the imagination might
be assisted to build a grander structure than the
Coliseum, and to shatter it with a more pictur-
esque decay. Byron's celebrated description is
better than the reality. He beheld the scene
in his mind's eye, through the witchery of many
intervening years, and faintly illuminated it as
if with starlight instead of this broad glow of
moonshine.

The party of our friends sat down, three or
four of them on a prostrate column, another on
a shapeless lump of marble, once a Roman altar;
others on the steps of one of the Christian shrines.
Goths and barbarians though they were, they
chatted as gaily together as if they belonged to
the gentle and pleasant race of people who now in-
habit Italy. There was much pastime and gaiety
just then in the area of the Coliseum, where
so many gladiators and wild beasts had fought
and died, and where so much blood of Christian
martyrs had been lapt up by that fiercest of wild

beasts, the Roman populace of yore. Some youths
and maidens were running merry races across the
open space, and playing at hide-and-seek a little
way within the duskiness of the ground-tier of
arches, whence now and then you could hear
the half-shriek, half-laugh, of a frolicksome girl,
whom the shadow had betrayed into a young
man's arms. Elder groups were seated on the
fragments of pillars and blocks of marble that
lay round the verge of the arena, talking in the
quick, short ripple of the Italian tongue. On
the steps of the great black cross in the centre
of the Coliseum, sat a party singing scraps of
songs, with much laughter and merriment be-
tween the stanzas.

It was a strange place for song and mirth.
That black cross marks one of the special blood-
spots of the earth, where thousands of times
over the dying gladiator fell, and more of human
agony has been endured for the mere pastime
of the multitude than on the breadth of many
battle-fields. From all this crime and suffering,

however, the spot has derived a more than com-
mon sanctity.   An inscription promises seven
years' indulgence, seven years of remission from
the pains of purgatory, and earlier enjoyment
of heavenly bliss, for each separate kiss imprinted
on the black cross.   What better use could be
made of life, after middle-age, when the accumu-
lated sins are many, and the remaining tempta-
tions few, than to spend it all in kissing the black
cross of the Coliseum!

Besides its central consecration, the whole area
has been made sacred by a range of shrines,
which are erected round the circle, each com-
memorating some scene or circumstance of the
Saviour's passion and suffering.   In accordance
with an ordinary custom, a pilgrim was making
his progress from shrine to shrine, upon his knees,
and saying a penitential prayer at each.   Light-
footed girls ran across the path along which he
crept, or sported with their friends close by the
shrines where he was kneeling.   The pilgrim
took no heed, and the girls meant no irreverence;

for in Italy religion jostles along side by side with business and sport, after a fashion of its own, and people are accustomed to kneel down and pray, or see others praying between two fits of merriment, or between two sins.

To make an end of our description, a red twinkle of light was visible amid the breadth of shadow that fell across the upper part of the Coliseum. Now it glimmered through a line of arches, or threw a broader gleam as it rose out of some profound abyss of ruin; now it was muffled by a heap of shrubbery which had adventurously clambered to that dizzy height; and so the red light kept ascending to loftier and loftier ranges of the structure, until it stood like a star where the blue sky rested against the Coliseum's topmost wall. It indicated a party of English or Americans paying the inevitable visit by moonlight, and exalting themselves with raptures that were Byron's, not their own.

Our company of artists sat on the fallen column, the pagan altar, and the steps of the Christian shrine, enjoying the moonlight and shadow, the present gaiety and the gloomy reminiscences of the scene, in almost equal share. Artists, indeed, are lifted by the ideality of their pursuits a little way off the earth, and are therefore able to catch the evanescent fragrance that floats in the atmosphere of life above the heads of the ordinary crowd. Even if they seem endowed with little imagination individually, yet there is a property, a gift, a talisman, common to their class, entitling them to partake somewhat more bountifully than other people in the thin delights of moonshine and romance.

"How delightful this is!" said Hilda; and she sighed for very pleasure.

"Yes," said Kenyon, who sat on the column, at her side. "The Coliseum is far more delightful, as we enjoy it now, than when eighty thousand persons sat squeezed together, row above row, to see their fellow-creatures torn by lions and tigers limb from limb. What a strange thought, that the Coliseum was really built for us, and has not

come to its best uses till almost two thousand
years after it was finished!"

"The Emperor Vespasian scarcely had us in
his mind," said Hilda, smiling, "but I thank him
none the less for building it."

"He gets small thanks, I fear, from the people
whose bloody instincts he pampered," rejoined
Kenyon. "Fancy a nightly assemblage of eighty
thousand melancholy and remorseful ghosts, look-
ing down from those tiers of broken arches, striv-
ing to repent of the savage pleasures which they
once enjoyed, but still longing to enjoy them over
again."

"You bring a Gothic horror into this peace-
ful moonlight scene," said Hilda.

"Nay, I have good authority for peopling
the Coliseum with phantoms," replied the sculp-
tor. "Do you remember that veritable scene
in Benvenuto Cellini's autobiography, in which a
necromancer of his acquaintance draws a magic
circle—just where the black cross stands now,
I suppose—and raises myriads of demons? Ben-

venuto saw them with his own eyes—giants,
pigmies, and other creatures of frightful aspect,
—capering and dancing on yonder walls. Those
spectres must have been Romans, in their life-
time, and frequenters of this bloody amphitheatre.

"I see a spectre now!" said Hilda, with a
little thrill of uneasiness. "Have you watched
that pilgrim, who is going round the whole
circle of shrines, on his knees, and praying with
such fervency at every one? Now that he has
revolved so far in his orbit, and has the moon-
shine on his face, as he turns towards us, me-
thinks I recognize him!"

"And so do I," said Kenyon. "Poor Miriam!
Do you think she sees him?"

They looked round, and perceived that Miriam
had risen from the steps of the shrine, and disap-
peared. She had shrunk back, in fact, into the
deep obscurity of an arch that opened just
behind them.

Donatello, whose faithful watch was no more
to be eluded than that of a hound, had stolen

after her, and became the innocent witness of a
spectacle that had its own kind of horror. Un-
aware of his presence, and fancying herself
wholly unseen, the beautiful Miriam began to
gesticulate extravagantly, gnashing her teeth,
flinging her arms wildly abroad, stamping with her
foot. It was as if she had stepped aside for
an instant, solely to snatch the relief of a
brief fit of madness. Persons in acute trouble,
or labouring under strong excitement, with a
necessity for concealing it, are prone to relieve
their nerves in this wild way; although, when
practicable, they find a more effectual solace in
shrieking aloud.

Thus, as soon as she threw off her self-con-
trol, under the dusky arches of the Coliseum,
we may consider Miriam as a mad woman, con-
centrating the elements of a long insanity into
that instant.

"Signorina! signorina! have pity on me!"
cried Donatello, approaching her—"this is too
terrible!"

"How dare you look at me?" exclaimed
Miriam, with a start; then, whispering below
her breath, "men have been struck dead for
a less offence!"

"If you desire it, or need it," said Dona-
tello, humbly, "I shall not be loth to die."

"Donatello," said Miriam, coming close to the
young man, and speaking low, but still the almost
insanity of the moment vibrating in her voice,
"if you love yourself, if you desire those earthly
blessings, such as you, of all men, were made for,
if you would come to a good old age among your
olive-orchards and your Tuscan vines, as your
forefathers did; if you would leave children to
enjoy the same peaceful, happy, innocent life,
then flee from me. Look not behind you! Get
you gone without another word." He gazed
sadly at her, but did not stir. "I tell you,"
Miriam went on, "there is a great evil hang-
ing over me! I know it; I see it in the sky;
I feel it in the air! It will overwhelm me as
utterly as if this arch should crumble down

upon our heads! It will crush you, too, if you
stand at my side! Depart, then; and make
the sign of the cross, as your faith bids you,
when an evil spirit is nigh. Cast me off, or
you are lost for ever."

A higher sentiment brightened upon Dona-
tello's face, than had hitherto seemed to belong
to its simple expression and sensuous beauty.

"I will never quit you," he said; "you can-
not drive me from you."

"Poor Donatello!" said Miriam, in a changed
tone, and rather to herself than him. "Is there
no other that seeks me out—follows me—is ob-
stinate to share my affliction and my doom—
but only you! They call me beautiful; and
I used to fancy that, at my need, I could bring
the whole world to my feet. And, lo! here is
my utmost need; and my beauty and my gifts
have brought me only this poor, simple boy.
Half-witted, they call him; and surely fit for
nothing but to be happy. And I accept his
aid! To-morrow, to-morrow, I will tell him

all!) Ah!) what a sin to stain his joyous na-
ture with the blackness of a woe like mine!"

She held out her hand to him, and smiled
sadly as Donatello pressed it to his lips. They
were now about to emerge from the depth of
the arch; but, just then, the kneeling pilgrim,
in his revolution round the orbit of the shrines,
had reached the one on the steps of which
Miriam had been sitting. There, as at the
other shrines, he prayed, or seemed to pray.
It struck Kenyon, however—who sat close by,
and saw his face distinctly—that the suppliant
was merely performing an enjoined penance,
and without the penitence that ought to have
given it effectual life. Even as he knelt, his
eyes wandered, and Miriam soon felt that he
had detected her, half hidden as she was within
the obscurity of the arch.

"He is evidently a good Catholic, however,"
whispered one of the party. "After all, I fear
we cannot identify him with the ancient pagan
who haunts the catacombs."

"The doctors of the Propaganda may have converted him," said another; "they have had fifteen hundred years to perform the task."

The company now deemed it time to continue their ramble. Emerging from a side entrance of the Coliseum, they had on their left the Arch of Constantine, and, above it, the shapeless ruins of the Palace of the Cæsars; portions of which have taken shape anew, in mediæval convents and modern villas. They turned their faces cityward, and, treading over the broad flagstones of the old Roman pavement, passed through the Arch of Titus. The moon shone brightly enough within it, to show the seven-branched Jewish candlestick, cut in the marble of the interior. The original of that awful trophy lies buried, at this moment, in the yellow mud of the Tiber; and, could its gold of Ophir again be brought to light, it would be the most precious relic of past ages, in the estimation of both Jew and Gentile.

Standing amid so much ancient dust, it is

difficult to spare the reader the commonplaces
of enthusiasm, on which hundreds of tourists
have already insisted. Over this half-worn
pavement, and beneath this Arch of Titus, the
Roman armies had trodden in their outward
march, to fight battles, a world's width away.
Returning victorious, with royal captives and
inestimable spoil, a Roman triumph, that most
gorgeous pageant of earthly pride, had streamed
and flaunted in hundred-fold succession over
these same flag-stones, and through this yet
stalwart archway. It is politic, however, to
make few allusions to such a past; nor, if we
would create an interest in the characters of
our story, is it wise to suggest how Cicero's
foot may have stepped on yonder stone, or
how Horace was wont to stroll near by, making
his footsteps chime with the measure of the ode
that was ringing in his mind. The very ghosts
of that massive and stately epoch have so much
density that the actual people of to-day seem
the thinner of the two, and stand more ghost-

like by the arches and columns, letting the rich sculpture be discerned through their ill-compacted substance.

The party kept onward, often meeting pairs and groups of midnight strollers like themselves. On such a moonlight night as this, Rome keeps itself awake and stirring, and is full of song and pastime, the noise of which mingles with your dreams, if you have gone betimes to bed. But it is better to be abroad, and take our own share of the enjoyable time; for the languor that weighs so heavily in the Roman atmosphere by day, is lightened beneath the moon and stars.

They had now reached the precincts of the Forum.

CHAPTER II.

ON THE EDGE OF A PRECIPICE.

"LET us settle it," said Kenyon, stamping his foot firmly down, "that this is precisely the spot where the chasm opened, into which Curtius precipitated his good steed and himself. Imagine the great, dusky gap, impenetrably deep, and with half-shaped monsters and hideous faces looming upward out of it, to the vast affright of the good citizens who peeped over the brim! There, now, is a subject, hitherto unthought of, for a grim and ghastly story, and, methinks, with a moral as deep as the gulf itself. Within it, beyond a question, there were prophetic visions—intimations of all the future calamities of Rome—shades of Goths and Gauls, and even of the French soldiers of to-day. It

was a pity to close it up so soon! I would
give much for a peep into such a chasm."

"I fancy," remarked Miriam, "that every per-
son takes a peep into it in moments of gloom and
despondency; that is to say, in his moments of
deepest insight."

"Where is it, then?" asked Hilda. "I never
peeped into it."

"Wait, and it will open for you," replied her
friend. "The chasm was merely one of the ori-
fices of that pit of blackness that lies beneath
us, everywhere. The firmest substance of human
happiness is but a thin crust spread over it, with
just reality enough to bear up the illusive stage-
scenery amid which we tread. It needs no earth-
quake to open the chasm. A footstep, a little
heavier than ordinary, will serve; and we must
step very daintily, not to break through the crust
at any moment. By-and-by, we inevitably sink!
It was a foolish piece of heroism in Curtius to
precipitate himself there, in advance; for all
Rome, you see, has been swallowed up in that

gulf, in spite of him. The Palace of the Cæsars has gone down thither, with a hollow, rumbling sound of its fragments! All the temples have tumbled into it; and thousands of statues have been thrown after! All the armies and the triumphs have marched into the great chasm, with their martial music playing, as they stept over the brink. All the heroes, the statesmen, and the poets! All piled upon poor Curtius, who thought to have saved them all! I am loth to smile at the self-conceit of that gallant horseman, but cannot well avoid it."

"It grieves me to hear you speak thus, Miriam," said Hilda, whose natural and cheerful piety was shocked by her friend's gloomy view of human destinies. "It seems to me that there is no chasm, nor any hideous emptiness under our feet, except what the evil within us digs. If there be such a chasm, let us bridge it over with good thoughts and deeds, and we shall tread safely to the other side. It was the guilt of Rome, no doubt, that caused this gulf to open; and Curtius filled it up with his heroic self-sacrifice and patriotism, which was the best virtue that the old Romans knew. Every wrong thing makes the gulf deeper; every right one helps to fill it up. As the evil of Rome was far more than its good, the whole commonwealth finally sank into it, indeed, but of no original necessity."

"Well, Hilda, it came to the same thing at last," answered Miriam despondingly.

"Doubtless, too," resumed the sculptor, (for his imagination was greatly excited by the idea of this wondrous chasm,) "all the blood that the Romans shed, whether on battle-fields, or in the Coliseum, or on the cross—in whatever public or private murder—ran into this fatal gulf, and formed a mighty subterranean lake of gore, right beneath our feet. The blood from the thirty wounds in Cæsar's breast flowed hitherward, and that pure little rivulet from Virginia's bosom, too! Virginia, beyond all question, was stabbed by her father, precisely where we are standing."

"Then the spot is hallowed for ever!" said Hilda.

"Is there such blessed potency in bloodshed?" asked Miriam. "Nay, Hilda, do not protest! I take your meaning rightly."

They again moved forward. And still, from the Forum and the Via Sacra, from beneath the arches of the Temple of Peace on one side, and the acclivity of the Palace of the Cæsars on the other, there arose singing voices of parties that were strolling through the moonlight. Thus, the air was full of kindred melodies that encountered one another, and twined themselves into a broad, vague music, out of which no single strain could be disentangled. These good examples, as well as the harmonious influences of the hour, incited our artist-friends to make proof of their own vocal powers. With what skill and breath they had, they set up a choral strain—"Hail, Columbia!" we believe—which those old Roman echoes must have found it exceeding difficult to repeat aright. Even Hilda poured the slender sweetness of her

note into her country's song. Miriam was at first
silent, being perhaps unfamiliar with the air and
burden. But, suddenly, she threw out such a
swell and gush of sound, that it seemed to pervade
the whole choir of other voices, and then to rise
above them all, and become audible in what would
else have been the silence of an upper region:
That volume of melodious voice was one of the
tokens of a great trouble. There had long been
an impulse upon her—amounting, at last, to a
necessity—to shriek aloud; but she had struggled
against it, till the thunderous anthem gave her
an opportunity to relieve her heart by a great
cry.

They passed the solitary column of Phocas, and
looked down into the excavated space, where a
confusion of pillars, arches, pavements, and shat-
tered blocks and shafts—the crumbs of various
ruin dropt from the devouring maw of Time—
stand, or lie, at the base of the Capitoline Hill.
That renowned hillock (for it is little more) now
rose abruptly above them. The ponderous ma-

sonry, with which the hill-side is built up, is as
old as Rome itself, and looks likely to endure
while the world retains any substance or per-
manence. It once sustained the Capitol, and now
bears up the great pile which the mediæval
builders raised on the antique foundation, and that
still loftier tower, which looks abroad upon a
larger page, of deeper historic interest, than any
other scene can show. On the same pedestal
of Roman masonry, other structures will doubt-
less rise, and vanish like ephemeral things.

To a spectator on the spot, it is remarkable
that the events of Roman history, and Roman
life itself, appear not so distant as the Gothic
ages which succeeded them. We stand in the
Forum, or on the height of the Capitol, and seem
to see the Roman epoch close at hand. We
forget that a chasm extends between it and our-
selves, in which lie all those dark, rude, unlettered
centuries, around the birth-time of Christianity,
as well as the age of chivalry and romance, the
feudal system, and the infancy of a better civiliza-

tion than that of Rome. Or, if we remember
these mediæval times, they look farther off than
the Augustan age. The reason may be, that the
old Roman literature survives, and creates for us
an intimacy with the classic ages, which we have
no means of forming with the subsequent ones.

The Italian climate, moreover, robs age of its
reverence, and makes it look newer than it is.
Not the Coliseum, nor the tombs of the Appian
Way, nor the oldest pillar in the Forum, nor
any other Roman ruin, be it as dilapidated as
it may, ever give the impression of venerable
antiquity which we gather, along with the ivy,
from the gray walls of an English abbey or
castle. And yet every brick or stone, which
we pick up among the former, had fallen, ages
before the foundation of the latter was begun.
This is owing to the kindliness with which Nature
takes an English ruin to her heart, covering it
with ivy, as tenderly as Robin Redbreast covered
the dead babes with forest leaves. She strives
to make it a part of herself, gradually obliterating

the handiwork of man, and supplanting it with
her own mosses and trailing verdure, till she has
won the whole structure back. But, in Italy,
whenever man has once hewn a stone, Nature
forthwith relinquishes her right to it, and never
lays her finger on it again. Age after age finds
it bare and naked, in the barren sunshine, and
leaves it so. Besides this natural disadvantage,
too, each succeeding century, in Rome, has done
its best to ruin the very ruins, so far as their
picturesque effect is concerned, by stealing away
the marble and hewn stone, and leaving only
yellow bricks, which never can look venerable.

The party ascended the winding way that leads
from the Forum to the Piazza of the Campidoglio
on the summit of the Capitoline Hill. They
stood awhile to contemplate the bronze equestrian
statue of Marcus Aurelius. The moonlight glis-
tened upon traces of the gilding which had once
covered both rider and steed; these were almost
gone, but the aspect of dignity was still perfect,
clothing the figure as it were with an imperial

robe of light. It is the most majestic representa-
tion of the kingly character that ever the world
has seen. A sight of the old heathen Emperor
is enough to create an evanescent sentiment of
loyalty even in a democratic bosom, so august
does he look, so fit to rule, so worthy of man's
profoundest homage and obedience, so inevitably
attractive of his love. He stretches forth his
hand with an air of grand beneficence and un-
limited authority, as if uttering a decree from
which no appeal was permissible, but in which
the obedient subject would find his highest inter-
ests consulted; a command, that was in itself a
benediction.

"The sculptor of this statue knew what a king
should be," observed Kenyon, "and knew, likewise,
the heart of mankind, and how it craves a true
ruler, under whatever title, as a child its father."

"Oh, if there were but one such man as this!"
exclaimed Miriam. "One such man in an age,
and one in all the world; then how speedily would
the strife, wickedness, and sorrow of us poor crea-

tures be relieved.? We would come to him with
our griefs, whatever they might be—even a poor,
frail woman burdened with her heavy heart—and
lay them at his feet, and never need to take them
up again. The rightful king would see to all."

"What an idea of the regal office and duty!"
said Kenyon, with a smile. "It is a woman's
idea of the whole matter, to perfection. It is
Hilda's too, no doubt?"

"No," answered the quiet Hilda,; "I should
never look for such assistance from an earthly
king."

"Hilda, my religious Hilda," whispered Mi-
riam, suddenly drawing the girl close to her,
"do you know how it is with me? I would give
all I have or hope—my life, oh, how freely,—for
one instant of your trust in God! You little guess
my need of it. You really think, then, that He
sees and cares for us?"

"Miriam, you frighten me."

"Hush, hush! do not let them hear you!"
whispered Miriam. "I frighten you, you say?

for Heaven's sake, how?   Am I strange? is there
anything wild in my behaviour?"

"Only for that moment," replied Hilda, "be-
cause you seemed to doubt God's providence."

"We will talk of that another time," said her
friend.   "Just now it is very dark to me."

On the left of the Piazza of the Campidoglio,
as you face cityward, and at the head of the long
and stately flight of steps, descending from the
Capitoline Hill to the level of lower Rome, there
is a narrow lane or passage.   Into this the party
of our friends now turned.   The path ascended
a little and ran along under the walls of a palace,
but soon passed through a gateway, and termi-
nated in a small paved courtyard.   It was bordered
by a low parapet.

The spot, for some reason or other, impressed
them as exceedingly lonely.   On one side was
the great height of the palace, with the moon-
shine falling over it, and showing all the windows
barred and shuttered.   Not a human eye could look
down into the little courtyard, even if the seem-

ingly deserted palace had a tenant. On all other
sides of its narrow compass there was nothing
but the parapet, which as it now appeared was
built right on the edge of a steep precipice.
Gazing from its imminent brow, the party be-
held a crowded confusion of roofs spreading over
the whole space between them and the line of
hills that lay beyond the Tiber. A long, misty
wreath just dense enough to catch a little of the
moonshine floated above the houses midway to-
wards the hilly line, and showed the course of
the unseen river. Far away on the right, the
moon gleamed on the dome of St. Peter's as well
as on many lesser and nearer domes.

"What a beautiful view of the city!" ex-
claimed Hilda; "and I never saw Rome from
this point before."

"It ought to afford a good prospect," said the
sculptor; "for it was from this point—at least
we are at liberty to think so, if we choose—that
many a famous Roman caught his last glimpse
of his native city, and of all other earthly things.

This is one of the sides of the Tarpeian Rock. Look over the parapet and see what a sheer tumble there might still be for a traitor, in spite of the thirty feet of soil that have accumulated at the foot of the precipice."

They all bent over, and saw that the cliff fell perpendicularly downward to about the depth, or rather more, at which the tall palace rose in height above their heads. Not that it was still the natural, shaggy front of the original precipice; for it appeared to be cased in ancient stone-work, through which the primeval rock showed its face here and there grimly and doubtfully. Mosses grew on the slight projections, and little shrubs sprouted out of the crevices, but could not much soften the stern aspect of the cliff. Brightly as the Italian moonlight fell a-down the height, it scarcely showed what portion of it was man's work, and what was Nature's, but left it all in very much the same kind of ambiguity and half-knowledge in which antiquarians generally leave the identity of Roman remains.

The roofs of some poor-looking houses which had been built against the base and sides of the cliff, rose nearly midway to the top; but from an angle of the parapet there was a precipitous plunge straight downward into a stone-paved court.

"I prefer this to any other site as having been veritably the Traitor's Leap," said Kenyon, "because it was so convenient to the Capitol. It was an admirable idea of those stern old fellows to fling their political criminals down from the very summit on which stood the Senate House and Jove's temple, emblems of the institutions which they sought to violate. It symbolizes how sudden was the fall in those days from the utmost height of ambition to its profoundest ruin."

"Come, come; it is midnight," cried another artist; "too late to be moralizing here. We are literary dreaming on the edge of a precipice. Let us go home."

"It is time, indeed," said Hilda.

The sculptor was not without hopes that he

might be favoured with the sweet charge of
escorting Hilda to the foot of her tower. Ac-
cordingly, when the party prepared to turn back,
he offered her his arm. · Hilda at first accepted
it; but when they had partly threaded the pas-
sage between the little courtyard and the Piazza
del Campidoglio, she discovered that Miriam had
remained behind.

"I must go back," said she, withdrawing her
arm from Kenyon's; "but pray do not come
with me. Several times this evening I have had
a fancy that Miriam had something on her mind,
some sorrow or perplexity, which, perhaps, it
would relieve her to tell me about. No, no;
do not turn back! Donatello will be a sufficient
guardian for Miriam and me."

The sculptor was a good deal mortified, and
perhaps a little angry; but he knew Hilda's
mood of gentle decision and independence too
well not to obey her. He therefore suffered the
fearless maiden to return alone.

Meanwhile, Miriam had not noticed the depar-

ture of the rest of the company; she remained
on the edge of the precipice, and Donatello along
with her.

"It would be a fatal fall, still," she said to
herself, looking over the parapet, and shuddering
as her eye measured the depth. "Yes; surely,
yes! Even without the weight of an over-
burdened heart, a human body would fall heavily
enough upon those stones to shake all its joints
asunder. How soon it would be over!"

Donatello, of whose presence she was possibly
not aware, now pressed closer to her side; and
he, too, like Miriam, bent over the low parapet
and trembled violently. Yet he seemed to feel
that perilous fascination which haunts the brow
of precipices, tempting the unwary one to fling
himself over, for the very horror of the thing;
for, after drawing hastily back, he again looked
down, thrusting himself out farther than before.
He then stood silent a brief space, struggling,
perhaps, to make himself conscious of the historic
associations of the scene.

" What are you thinking of, Donatello?" asked
Miriam.

" Who were they," said he, looking earnestly
in her face, " who have been flung over here in
days gone by?"

" Men that cumbered the world," she replied.
" Men whose lives were the bane of their fellow-
creatures. Men who poisoned the air, which is
the common breath of all, for their own selfish
purposes. There was short work with such men
in old Roman times. Just in the moment of
their triumph a hand, as of an avenging giant,
clutched them, and dashed the wretches down this
precipice."

" Was it well done?" asked the young man.

" It was well done," answered Miriam; " inno-
cent persons were saved by the destruction of
a guilty one, who deserved his doom."

While this brief conversation passed, Donatello
had once or twice glanced aside with a watchful
air, just as a hound may often be seen to take
sidelong note of some suspicious object, while he

gives his more direct attention to something
nearer at hand. Miriam seemed now first to
become aware of the silence that had followed
upon the cheerful talk and laughter of a few
moments before. Looking round, she perceived
that all her company of merry friends had re-
tired, and Hilda, too, in whose soft and quiet
presence she had always an indescribable feel-
ing of security. All gone; and only herself and
Donatello left hanging over the brow of the
ominous precipice.

Not so, however; not entirely alone! In the
basement wall of the palace, shaded from the
moon, there was a deep, empty niche, that had
probably once contained a statue; not empty,
either; for a figure now came forth from it,
and approached Miriam. She must have had
cause to dread some unspeakable evil from this
strange persecutor, and to know that this was
the very crisis of her calamity; for, as he drew
near, such a cold, sick despair crept over her,
that it impeded her breath, and benumbed her

natural promptitude of thought. Miriam seemed
dreamily to remember falling on her knees; but,
in her whole recollection of that wild moment,
she beheld herself as in a dim show, and could
not well distinguish what was done and suffered;
no, not even whether she were really an actor and
sufferer in the scene.

Hilda, meanwhile, had separated herself from
the sculptor, and turned back to rejoin her friend.
At a distance, she still heard the mirth of her late
companions, who were going down the cityward
descent of the Capitoline Hill; they had set up
a new stave of melody, in which her own soft
voice, as well as the powerful sweetness of
Miriam's, was sadly missed.

The door of the little courtyard had swung
upon its hinges, and partly closed itself. Hilda
(whose native gentleness pervaded all her move-
ments) was quietly opening it, when she was
startled, midway, by the noise of a struggle
within, beginning and ending all in one breathless
instant. Along with it, or closely succeeding it,

was a loud, fearful cry, which quivered upward
through the air, and sank quivering downward
to the earth. Then, a silence! Poor Hilda had
looked into the courtyard, and saw the whole
quick passage of a deed, which took but that
little time to grave itself in the eternal adamant.

CHAPTER III.

THE FAUN'S TRANSFORMATION.

THE door of the courtyard swung slowly, and closed itself of its own accord. Miriam and Donatello were now alone there. She clasped her hands, and looked wildly at the young man, whose form seemed to have dilated, and whose eyes blazed with the fierce energy that had suddenly inspired him. It had kindled him into a man; it had developed within him an intelligence which was no native characteristic of the Donatello whom we have heretofore known. But that simple and joyous creature was gone for ever.

"What have you done?" said Miriam, in a horror-stricken whisper.

The glow of rage was still lurid on Donatello's face, and now flashed out again from his eyes.

"I did what ought to be done to a traitor!"
he replied. "I did what your eyes bade me do,
when I asked them with mine, as I held the
wretch over the precipice!"

These last words struck Miriam like a bullet.
Could it be so? Had her eyes provoked, or
assented to this deed? She had not known it.
But, alas! looking back into the frenzy and
turmoil of the scene just acted, she could not
deny—she was not sure whether it might be so,
or no—that a wild joy had flamed up in her
heart, when she beheld her persecutor in his
mortal peril. Was it horror?—or ecstasy?—or
both in one? Be the emotion what it might,
it had blazed up more madly, when Donatello
flung his victim off the cliff, and more and more,
while his shriek went quivering downward. With
the dead thump upon the stones below, had come
an unutterable horror.

"And my eyes bade you do it!" repeated
she.

They both leaned over the parapet, and gazed

downward as earnestly as if some inestimable
treasure had fallen over, and were yet recover-
able. On the pavement, below, was a dark mass,
lying in a heap, with little or nothing human in
its appearance, except that the hands were
stretched out, as if they might have clutched,
for a moment, at the small square stones. But
there was no motion in them, now. Miriam
watched the heap of mortality while she could
count a hundred, which she took pains to do. No
stir; not a finger moved.

"You have killed him, Donatello! He is quite
dead!" said she. "Stone dead! Would I were
so, too!"

"Did you not mean that he should die?"
sternly asked Donatello, still in the glow of that
intelligence which passion had developed in him.
"There was short time to weigh the matter; but
he had his trial in that breath or two, while I held
him over the cliff, and his sentence in that one
glance, when your eyes responded to mine! Say
that I have slain him against your will—say that

he died without your whole consent—and, in
another breath, you shall see me lying beside
him."

"Oh, never!" cried Miriam. "My one, own
friend! Never, never, never!"

She turned to him—the guilty, blood-stained,
lonely woman—she turned to her fellow-criminal,
the youth, so lately innocent, whom she had
drawn into her doom. She pressed him close, close
to her bosom, with a clinging embrace that
brought their two hearts together, till the horror
and agony of each was combined into one emotion,
and that, a kind of rapture.

"Yes, Donatello, you speak the truth!" said
she; "my heart consented to what you did. We
two slew yonder wretch. The deed knots us
together for time and eternity, like the coil of
a serpent!"

They threw one other glance at the heap of
death below, to assure themselves that it was
there; so like a dream was the whole thing.
Then they turned from that fatal precipice, and

came out of the courtyard, arm in arm, heart
in heart. Instinctively, they were heedful not
to sever themselves so much as a pace or two
from one another, for fear of the terror and
deadly chill that would thenceforth wait for them
in solitude. Their deed—the crime which Dona-
tello wrought, and Miriam accepted on the instant
—had wreathed itself, as she said, like a serpent,
in inextricable links about both their souls, and
drew them into one, by its terrible contractile
power. It was closer than a marriage-bond. So
intimate, in those first moments, was the union
that it seemed as if their new sympathy annihi-
lated all other ties, and that they were released
from the chain of humanity; a new sphere, a
special law, had been created for them alone.
The world could not come near them; they were
safe !

When they reached the flight of steps, leading
downward from the Capitol, there was a far-off
noise of singing and laughter. Swift, indeed, had
been the rush of the crisis that was come and

gone! This was still the merriment of the party
that had so recently been their companions; they
recognized the voices which, a little while ago,
had accorded and sung in cadence with their own.
But they were familiar voices no more; they
sounded strangely, and, as it were, out of the
depths of space; so remote was all that per-
tained to the past life of these guilty ones, in
the moral seclusion that had suddenly extended
itself around them. But how close, and ever
closer, did the breadth of the immeasurable
waste, that lay between them and all brother-
hood or sisterhood, now press them one within
the other!

"Oh, friend," cried Miriam, so putting her
soul into that word that it took a heavy richness
of meaning, and seemed never to have been
spoken before. "Oh, friend, are you conscious,
as I am, of this companionship that knits our
heart-strings together?"

"I feel it, Miriam," said Donatello. "We
draw one breath; we live one life!"

"Only yesterday," continued Miriam; "nay, only a short half-hour ago, I shivered in an icy solitude. No friendship, no sisterhood, could come near enough to keep the warmth within my heart. In an instant, all is changed! There can be no more loneliness!"

"None, Miriam!" said Donatello.

"None, my beautiful one!" responded Miriam, gazing in his face, which had taken a higher, almost an heroic aspect from the strength of passion. "None, my innocent one! Surely, it is no crime that we have committed. One wretched and worthless life has been sacrificed, to cement two other lives for evermore."

"For evermore, Miriam!" said Donatello; "cemented with his blood!"

The young man started at the word which he had himself spoken; it may be that it brought home, to the simplicity of his imagination, what he had not before dreamed of—the ever-increasing loathsomeness of a union that consists in guilt. Cemented with blood, which would corrupt and grow more noisome for ever and for ever, but bind them none the less strictly for that!

"Forget it! Cast it all behind you!" said Miriam, detecting, by her sympathy, the pang that was in his heart. "The deed has done its office, and has no existence any more."

They flung the past behind them, as she counselled, or else distilled from it a fiery intoxication, which sufficed to carry them triumphantly through those first moments of their doom. For, guilt has its moment of rapture too. The foremost result of a broken law is ever an ecstatic sense of freedom. And thus there exhaled upward (out of their dark sympathy, at the base of which lay a human corpse) a bliss, or an insanity, which the unhappy pair imagined to be well worth the sleepy innocence that was for ever lost to them.

As their spirits rose to the solemn madness of the occasion, they went onward—not stealthily, not fearfully—but with a stately gait and aspect. Passion lent them (as it does to meaner shapes) its brief nobility of carriage. They trode through the streets of Rome, as if they, too, were among the majestic and guilty shadows, that, from ages long gone by, have haunted the blood-stained city. And, at Miriam's suggestion, they turned aside, for the sake of treading loftily past the old site of Pompey's forum.

"For there was a great deed done here!" she said—"a deed of blood, like ours! Who knows, but we may meet the high and ever-sad fraternity of Cæsar's murderers, and exchange a salutation?"

"Are they our brethren, now?" asked Donatello.

"Yes; all of them," said Miriam; "and many another, whom the world little dreams of, has been made our brother or our sister, by what we have done within this hour!"

And, at the thought, she shivered. Where, then, was the seclusion, the remoteness, the strange, lonesome Paradise, into which she and her one companion had been transported by their

crime? Was there, indeed, no such refuge, but
only a crowded thoroughfare and jostling throng
of criminals? And was it true, that whatever
hand had a blood-stain on it—or had poured out
poison—or strangled a babe at its birth—or clutched
a grandsire's throat, he sleeping, and robbed him
of his few last breaths—had now the right to offer
itself in fellowship with their two hands? Too
certainly, that right existed. It is a terrible
thought, that an individual wrong-doing melts
into the great mass of human crime, and makes
us—who dreamed only of our own little separate
sin—makes us guilty of the whole. And thus
Miriam and her lover were not an insulated pair,
but members of an innumerable confraternity of
guilty ones, all shuddering at each other.

"But not now; not yet," she murmured to
herself. "To-night, at least, there shall be no
remorse!"

Wandering without a purpose, it so chanced
that they turned into a street, at one extremity
of which stood Hilda's tower. There was a light

in her high chamber; a light, too, at the Virgin's
shrine; and the glimmer of these two was the
loftiest light beneath the stars. Miriam drew Do-
natello's arm to make him stop, and while they
stood at some distance looking at Hilda's window,
they beheld her approach and throw it open. She
leaned far forth, and extended her clasped hands
towards the sky.

"The good, pure child! She is praying, Do-
natello," said Miriam, with a kind of simple joy
at witnessing the devoutness of her friend. Then
her own sin rushed upon her, and she shouted,
with the rich strength of her voice, "Pray for
us, Hilda; we need it!"

Whether Hilda heard and recognized the voice
we cannot tell. The window was immediately
closed, and her form disappeared from behind the
snowy curtain. Miriam felt this to be a token
that the cry of her condemned spirit was shut
out of heaven.

CHAPTER IV.

THE BURIAL CHAUNT.

THE Church of the Capuchins (where, as the reader may remember, some of our acquaintances had made an engagement to meet) stands a little aside from the Piazza Barberini. Thither, at the hour agreed upon on the morning after the scenes last described, Miriam and Donatello directed their steps. At no time are people so sedulously careful to keep their trifling appointments, attend to their ordinary occupations, and thus put a commonplace aspect on life, as when conscious of some secret that if suspected would make them look monstrous in the general eye.

Yet how tame and wearisome is the impression of all ordinary things in the contrast with such a fact! How sick and tremulous, the next

morning, is the spirit that has dared so much,
only the night before! How icy cold is the
heart, when the fervour, the wild ecstasy of pas-
sion has faded away, and sunk down among the
dead ashes of the fire that blazed so fiercely, and
was fed by the very substance of its life! How
faintly does the criminal stagger onward, lacking
the impulse of that strong madness that hurried
him into guilt, and treacherously deserts him in
the midst of it!

When Miriam and Donatello drew near the
church, they found only Kenyon awaiting them
on the steps. Hilda had likewise promised to
be of the party, but had not yet appeared. Meet-
ing the sculptor, Miriam put a force upon her-
self, and succeeded in creating an artificial flow
of spirits, which to any but the nicest observation
was quite as effective as a natural one. She
spoke sympathizingly to the sculptor on the sub-
ject of Hilda's absence, and somewhat annoyed
him by alluding, in Donatello's hearing, to an
attachment which had never been openly avowed,

though perhaps plainly enough betrayed. He
fancied that Miriam did not quite recognize the
limits of the strictest delicacy; he even went
so far as to generalize, and conclude within him-
self that this deficiency is a more general failing
in woman than in man, the highest refinement
being a masculine attribute.

But the idea was unjust to the sex at large,
and especially so to this poor Miriam, who was
hardly responsible for her frantic efforts to be
gay. Possibly, moreover, the nice action of the
mind is set ajar by any violent shock, as of great
misfortune or great crime, so that the finer percep-
tions may be blurred thenceforth, and the effect be
traceable in all the minutest conduct of life.

"Did you see anything of the dear child after
you left us?" asked Miriam, still keeping Hilda
as her topic of conversation. "I missed her
sadly on my way homeward; for nothing ensures
me such delightful and innocent dreams (I have
experienced it twenty times) as a talk late in
the evening with Hilda."

"So I should imagine," said the sculptor, gravely; "but it is an advantage that I have little or no opportunity of enjoying. I know not what became of Hilda after my parting from you. She was not especially my companion in any part of our walk. The last I saw of her, she was hastening back to rejoin you in the court-yard of the Palazzo Caffarelli."

"Impossible!" cried Miriam, starting.

"Then did you not see her again?" inquired Kenyon, in some alarm.

"Not there," answered Miriam, quietly, "in-deed, I followed pretty closely on the heels of the rest of the party. But do not be alarmed on Hilda's account; the Virgin is bound to watch over the good child, for the sake of the piety with which she keeps the lamp alight at her shrine. And, besides, I have always felt that Hilda is just as safe in these evil streets of Rome as her white doves when they fly downwards from the tower-top, and run to and fro among the horses' feet. There is certainly a providence

or purpose for Hilda, if for no other human crea-
ture."

"I religiously believe it," rejoined the sculp-
tor; "and yet my mind would be the easier,
if I knew that she had returned safely to her
tower."

"Then make yourself quite easy," answered
Miriam. "I saw her (and it is the last sweet
sight that I remember) leaning from her window
midway between earth and sky!"

Kenyon now looked at Donatello.

"You seem out of spirits, my dear friend,"
he observed. "This languid Roman atmosphere
is not the airy wine that you were accustomed
to breathe at home. I have not forgotten your
hospitable invitation to meet you this summer
at your castle among the Apennines. It is my
fixed purpose to come, I assure you. We shall
both be the better for some deep draughts of the
mountain-breezes."

"It may be," said Donatello, with unwonted
sombreness; "the old house seemed joyous when

I was a child. But as I remember it now it was a grim place, too."

The sculptor looked more attentively at the young man, and was surprised and alarmed to observe how entirely the fine, fresh glow of animal spirits had departed out of his face. Hitherto, moreover, even while he was standing perfectly still, there had been a kind of possible gambol indicated in. his aspect. It was quite gone now. All his youthful gaiety, and with it his simplicity of manner, was eclipsed, if not utterly extinct.

"You are surely ill, my dear fellow," exclaimed Kenyon.

"Am I? Perhaps so," said Donatello, indifferently; "I never have been ill, and know not what it may be."

"Do not make the poor lad fancy-sick," whispered Miriam, pulling the sculptor's sleeve. "He is of a nature to lie down and die at once, if he finds himself drawing such melancholy breaths as we ordinary people are enforced to burden

our lungs withal. But we must get him away
from this old, dreamy, and dreary Rome, where
nobody but himself ever thought of being gay.
Its influences are too heavy to sustain the life
of such a creature."

The above conversation had passed chiefly on
the steps of the Cappuccini; and, having said
so much, Miriam lifted the leathern curtain that
hangs before all church doors in Italy.

"Hilda has forgotten her appointment," she
observed, "or else her maiden slumbers are
very sound this morning. We will wait for
her no longer."

They entered the nave. The interior of the
church was of moderate compass, but of good
architecture, with a vaulted roof over the nave,
and a row of dusky chapels on either side of it
instead of the customary side-aisles. Each chapel
had its saintly shrine, hung round with offer-
ings; its picture above the altar, although closely
veiled, if by any painter of renown; and its
hallowed tapers, burning continually, to set

alight the devotion of the worshippers. The
pavement of the nave was chiefly of marble,
and looked old and broken, and was shabbily
patched here and there with tiles of brick; it
was inlaid, moreover, with tombstones of the
mediæval taste, on which were quaintly sculp-
tured borders, figures, and portraits in bas-relief,
and Latin epitaphs, now grown illegible by the
tread of footsteps over them. The church ap-
pertains to a convent of Capuchin monks; and,
as usually happens when a reverend brother-
hood have such an edifice in charge, the floor
seemed never to have been scrubbed or swept,
and had as little the aspect of sanctity as a
kennel; whereas, in all churches of nunneries,
the maiden sisterhood invariably show the purity
of their own hearts by the virgin cleanliness
and visible consecration of the walls and pave-
ment.

As our friends entered the church, their eyes
rested at once on a remarkable object in the
centre of the nave. It was either the actual

body,) or, as might rather have been supposed
at first glance, the cunningly wrought waxen
face and suitably draped figure of a dead monk.
This image of wax or clay-cold reality, which-
ever it might be, lay on a slightly elevated
bier, with three tall candles burning on each
side, another tall candle at the head, and an-
other at the foot. There was music, too, in
harmony with so funereal a spectacle. From be-
neath the pavement of the church came the
deep, lugubrious strain of a *De Profundis,*
which sounded like an utterance of the tomb
itself; so dismally did it rumble through the
burial-vaults, and ooze up among the flat grave-
stones and sad epitaphs, filling the church as
with a gloomy mist.

" I must look more closely at that dead monk
before we leave the church," remarked the sculp-
tor. " In the study of my art, I have gained
many a hint from the dead, which the living
could never have given me."

" I can well imagine it," answered Miriam,

"One clay image is readily copied from another. But let us first see Guido's picture. The light is favourable now."

Accordingly, they turned into the first chapel on the right hand, as you enter the nave; and there they beheld—not the picture, indeed—but a closely drawn curtain. The churchmen of Italy make no scruple of sacrificing the very purpose for which a work of sacred art has been created, that of opening the way for religious sentiment through the quick medium of sight, by bringing angels, saints, and martyrs, down visibly upon earth; of sacrificing this high purpose, and, for aught they know, the welfare of many souls along with it, to the hope of a paltry fee. Every work by an artist of celebrity is hidden behind a veil, and seldom revealed except to Protestants, who scorn it as an object of devotion, and value it only for its artistic merit.

The sacristan was quickly found, however, and lost no time in disclosing the youthful Arch-

angel, setting his divine foot on the head of his
fallen adversary. It was an image of that
greatest of future events, which we hope for so
ardently, at least, while we are young, but)
find so very long in coming—the triumph of
goodness over the evil principle.

"Where can Hilda be?" exclaimed Kenyon.
"It is not her custom ever to fail in an en-
gagement; and the present one was made en-
tirely on her account. Except herself, you know,
we were all agreed in our recollection of the
picture."

"But we were wrong, and Hilda right, as
you perceive," said Miriam, directing his atten-
tion to the point on which their dispute of the
night before had arisen. "It is not easy to
detect her astray, as regards any picture on
which those clear, soft eyes of hers have ever
rested."

"And she has studied and admired few pic-
tures so much as this," observed the sculptor.
"No wonder; for there is hardly another so

beautiful in the world. What an expression of heavenly severity in the Archangel's face! There is a degree of pain, trouble, and disgust at being brought in contact with sin, even for the purpose of quelling and punishing it; and yet a celestial tranquillity pervades his whole being."

"I have never been able," said Miriam, "to admire this picture nearly so much as Hilda does, in its moral and intellectual aspect. If it cost her more trouble to be good, if her soul were less white and pure, she would be a more competent critic of this picture, and would estimate it not half so high. I see its defects to-day more clearly than ever before."

"What are some of them?" asked Kenyon.

"That Archangel, now," Miriam continued, "how fair he looks, with his unruffled wings, with his unhacked sword, and clad in his bright armour, and that exquisitely fitting sky-blue tunic, cut in the latest Paradisaical mode! What a dainty air of the first celestial society! With what half-scornful delicacy he sets his prettily

sandalled foot on the head of his prostrate foe!
But, is it thus that virtue looks, the moment
after its death-struggle with evil? No, no! I
could have told Guido better. A full third
of the Archangel's feathers should have been
torn from his wings; the rest all ruffled, till
they looked like Satan's own! His sword should
be streaming with blood, and perhaps broken
half way to the hilt; his armour crushed, his
robes rent, his breast gory; a bleeding gash on
his brow, cutting right across the stern scowl
of battle! He should press his foot hard down
upon the old serpent, as if his very soul de-
pended upon it, feeling him squirm mightily,
and doubting whether the fight were half over
yet, and how the victory might turn! And,
with all this fierceness, this grimness, this un-
utterable horror, there should still be something
high, tender, and holy, in Michael's eyes, and
around his mouth. But the battle never was
such child's play as Guido's dapper Archangel
seems to have found it."

"For Heaven's sake, Miriam," cried Kenyon, astonished at the wild energy of her talk; "paint the picture of man's struggle against sin according to your own idea! I think it will be a masterpiece."

"The picture would have its share of truth, I assure you," she answered; "but I am sadly afraid the victory would fall on the wrong side. Just fancy a smoke-blackened, fiery-eyed demon, bestriding that nice young angel, clutching his white throat with one of his hinder claws; and giving a triumphant whisk of his scaly tail, with a poisonous dart at the end of it! That is what they risk, poor souls, who do battle with Michael's enemy."

It now, perhaps, struck Miriam that her mental disquietude was impelling her to an undue vivacity; for she paused, and turned away from the picture, without saying a word more about it. All this while, moreover, Donatello had been very ill at ease, casting awe-stricken and inquiring glances at the dead monk; as if

when forced upon the contemplation of a person
so naturally joyous as Donatello, who lived
with completeness in the present moment, and
was able to form but vague images of the future.

"What is the matter, Donatello?" whispered Miriam, soothingly. "You are quite in
a tremble, my poor friend! What is it?"

"This awful chaunt from beneath the church,"
answered Donatello; "it oppresses me; the air
is so heavy with it that I can scarcely draw
my breath. And yonder dead monk! I feel
as if he were lying right across my heart."

"Take courage!" whispered she again, "come;
we will approach close to the dead monk. The
only way, in such cases, is to stare the ugly
horror right in the face; never a side-long
glance, nor a half-look, for those are what

strong for both of us. Be brave; and all is well."

Donatello hung back for a moment, but then pressed close to Miriam's side, and suffered her to lead him up to the bier. The sculptor followed. A number of persons, chiefly women, with several children among them, were standing about the corpse; and as our three friends drew nigh, a mother knelt down, and caused her little boy to kneel, both kissing the beads and crucifix that hung from the monk's girdle. Possibly he had died in the odour of sanctity; or, at all events, death and his brown frock and cowl made a sacred image of this reverend father.

CHAPTER V.

THE DEAD CAPUCHIN.

THE dead monk was clad, as when alive, in the
brown woollen frock of the Capuchins, with the
hood drawn over his head, but so as to leave the
features and a portion of the beard uncovered.
His rosary and cross hung at his side; his hands
were folded over his breast; his feet (he was of
a bare-footed order in his lifetime, and con-
tinued so in death) protruded from beneath his
habit, stiff and stark, with a more waxen look
than even his face. They were tied together at
the ankles with a black ribbon.

The countenance, as we have already said, was
fully displayed. It had a purplish hue upon it,
unlike the paleness of an ordinary corpse, but as
little resembling the flush of natural life. The

eyelids were but partially drawn down, and
showed the eyeballs beneath; as if the deceased
friar were stealing a glimpse at the bystanders,
to watch whether they were duly impressed with
the solemnity of his obsequies. The shaggy eye-
brows gave sternness to the look.

Miriam passed between two of the lighted
candles, and stood close beside the bier.

"My God!" murmured she. "What is
this?"

She grasped Donatello's hand, and, at the same
instant, felt him give a convulsive shudder,
which she knew to have been caused by a sud-
den and terrible throb of the heart. His hand,
by an instantaneous change, became like ice
within hers, which likewise grew so icy, that
their insensible fingers might have rattled, one
against the other. No wonder that their blood
curdled; no wonder that their hearts leapt, and
paused! The dead face of the monk, gazing at
them beneath its half-closed eyelids, was the
same visage that had glared upon their naked

souls, the past midnight, as Donatello flung him
over the precipice.

The sculptor was standing at the foot of the
bier, and had not yet seen the monk's features.

"Those naked feet!" said he. "I know not
why, but they affect me strangely. They have
walked to and fro over the hard pavements of
Rome, and through a hundred other rough ways
of this life, where the monk went begging for
his brotherhood; along the cloisters and dreary
corridors of his convent, too, from his youth
upward! It is a suggestive idea, to track those
worn feet backward through all the paths they
have trodden, ever since they were the tender
and rosy little feet of a baby, and (cold as they
now are) were kept warm in his mother's hand."

As his companions, whom the sculptor sup-
posed to be close by him, made no response to
his fanciful musing, he looked up, and saw them
at the head of the bier. He advanced thither
himself.

"Ha!" exclaimed he.

man's sudden death. In truth, it seemed too wild a thought, to connect, in reality, Miriam's persecutor of many past months and the vagabond of the preceding night, with the dead Capuchin of to-day. It resembled one of those unaccountable changes and interminglings of identity, which so often occur among the personages of a dream. But Kenyon, as befitted the professor of an imaginative art, was endowed with an exceedingly quick sensibility, which was apt to give him intimations of the true state of matters that lay beyond his actual vision. There was a whisper in his ear; it said, "Hush!" Without asking himself wherefore, he resolved to be silent as regarded the mysterious discovery which he had made, and to leave any remark or explanation to be voluntarily offered by

23—2

Miriam. If she never spoke, then let the riddle be unsolved.

And now occurred a circumstance that would seem too fantastic to be told, if it had not actually happened, precisely as we set it down. As the three friends stood by the bier, they saw that a little stream of blood had begun to ooze from the dead monk's nostrils; it crept slowly towards the thicket of his beard, where, in the course of a moment or two, it hid itself.

"How strange!" ejaculated Kenyon. "The monk died of apoplexy, I suppose, or by some sudden accident, and the blood has not yet congealed."

"Do you consider that a sufficient explanation?" asked Miriam, with a smile from which the sculptor involuntarily turned away his eyes. "Does it satisfy you?"

"And why not?" he inquired.

"Of course, you know the old superstition about this phenomenon of blood flowing from a dead body," she rejoined. "How can we tell

but that the murderer of this monk (or, possibly,
it may be only that privileged murderer, his
physician) may have just entered the church?"

"I cannot jest about it," said Kenyon. "It
is an ugly sight!"

"True, true; horrible to see, or dream of!"
she replied, with one of those long, tremulous
sighs, which so often betray a sick heart by
escaping unexpectedly. "We will not look at
it any more. Come away, Donatello. Let us
escape from this dismal church. The sunshine
will do you good."

When had ever a woman such a trial to sus-
tain as this! By no possible supposition, could
Miriam explain the identity of the dead Capu-
chin, quietly and decorously laid out in the nave
of his convent church, with that of her murdered
persecutor, flung heedlessly at the foot of the
precipice. The effect upon her imagination was
as if a strange and unknown corpse had mira-
culously, while she was gazing at it, assumed
the likeness of that face, so terrible henceforth

in her remembrance. It was a symbol, perhaps, of the deadly iteration with which she was doomed to behold the image of her crime reflected back upon her in a thousand ways, and converting the great, calm face of Nature, in the whole, and in its innumerable details, into a manifold reminiscence of that one dead visage.

No sooner had Miriam turned away from the bier, and gone a few steps, than she fancied the likeness altogether an illusion, which would vanish at a closer and colder view. She must look at it again, therefore, and at once; or else the grave would close over the face, and leave the awful fantasy that had connected itself therewith, fixed ineffaceably in her brain.

"Wait for me, one moment!" she said to her companions. "Only a moment!"

So she went back, and gazed once more at the corpse. Yes; these were the features that Miriam had known so well; this was the visage that she remembered from a far longer date than the most intimate of her friends suspected; this

form of clay had held the evil spirit which
blasted her sweet youth, and compelled her, as
it were, to stain her womanhood with crime.
But, whether it were the majesty of death, or
something originally noble and lofty in the
character of the dead, which the soul had
stamped upon the features, as it left them; so
it was that Miriam now quailed and shook, not
for the vulgar horror of the spectacle, but for
the severe, reproachful glance that seemed to
come from between those half-closed lids. True
there had been nothing, in his lifetime, viler
than this man. She knew it; there was no
other fact within her consciousness that she felt
to be so certain ; and yet, because her persecutor
found himself safe and irrefutable in death, he
frowned upon his victim, and threw back the
blame on her!

"Is it thou, indeed?" she murmured, under
her breath. "Then thou hast no right to scowl
upon me so! But art thou real, or a vision?"

She bent down over the dead monk, till one

of her rich curls brushed against his forehead.
She touched one of his folded hands with her
finger.

"It is he!" said Miriam. "There is the scar,
that I know so well, on his brow. And it is no
vision; he is palpable to my touch! I will
question the fact no longer, but deal with it as
I best can."

It was wonderful to see how the crisis developed
in Miriam its own proper strength, and the
faculty of sustaining the demands which it made
upon her fortitude. She ceased to tremble; the
beautiful woman gazed sternly at her dead
enemy, endeavouring to meet and quell the look
of accusation that he threw from between his
half-closed eyelids.

"No; thou shalt not scowl me down!" said
she. "Neither now, nor when we stand together
at the judgment-seat. I fear not to meet thee
there. Farewell, till that next encounter!"

Haughtily waving her hand, Miriam rejoined
her friends, who were awaiting her at the door

of the church. As they went out, the sacristan stopped them, and proposed to show the cemetery of the convent, where the deceased members of the fraternity are laid to rest in sacred earth, brought long ago from Jerusalem.

"And will yonder monk be buried there?" she asked.

"Brother Antonio?" exclaimed the sacristan. "Surely, our good brother will be put to bed there! His grave is already dug, and the last occupant has made room for him. Will you look at it, signorina?"

"I will!" said Miriam.

"Then excuse me," observed Kenyon; "for I shall leave you. One dead monk has more than sufficed me; and I am not bold enough to face the whole mortality of the convent."

It was easy to see, by Donatello's looks, that he, as well as the sculptor, would gladly have escaped a visit to the famous cemetery of the Cappuccini. But Miriam's nerves were strained to such a pitch, that she anticipated a certain

solace and absolute relief in passing from one
ghastly spectacle to another of long-accumulated
ugliness; and there was, besides, a singular sense
of duty which impelled her to look at the final
resting-place of the being whose fate had been
so disastrously involved with her own. She
therefore followed the sacristan's guidance, and
drew her companion along with her, whispering
encouragement as they went.

The cemetery is beneath the church, but
entirely above ground, and lighted by a row of
iron-grated windows without glass. A corridor
runs along beside these windows, and gives
access to three or four vaulted recesses, or
chapels, of considerable breadth and height, the
floor of which consists of the consecrated earth
of Jerusalem. It is smoothed decorously over
the deceased brethren of the convent, and is
kept quite free from grass or weeds, such as
would grow even in these gloomy recesses, if
pains were not bestowed to root them up. But,
as the cemetery is small, and it is a precious

privilege to sleep in holy ground, the brotherhood
are immemorially accustomed, when one of their
number dies, to take the longest-buried skeleton
out of the oldest grave, and lay the new slumberer
there instead. Thus, each of the good friars,
in his turn, enjoys the luxury of a consecrated
bed, attended with the slight drawback of being
forced to get up long before daybreak, as it
were, and make room for another lodger.

The arrangement of the unearthed skeletons is
what makes the special interest of the cemetery.
Tho arched and vaulted walls of the burial
recesses are supported by massive pillars and
pilasters made of thigh-bones and skulls; the
whole material of the structure appears to be
of a similar kind; and the knobs and embossed
ornaments of this strange architecture are repre-
sented by the joints of the spine, and the more
delicate tracery by the smaller bones of the
human frame. The summits of the arches are
adorned with entire skeletons, looking as if they
were wrought most skilfully in bas-relief. There

is no possibility of describing how ugly and
grotesque is the effect, combined with a certain
artistic merit, nor how much perverted ingenuity
has been shown in this queer way, nor what a
multitude of dead monks, through how many
hundred years, must have contributed their bony
framework to build up these great arches of
mortality. On some of the skulls there are in-
scriptions, purporting that such a monk, who
formerly made use of that particular head-piece,
died on such a day and year; but vastly the
greater number are piled up indistinguishably
into the architectural design like the many deaths
that make up the one glory of a victory.

In the side walls of the vaults are niches where
skeleton monks sit or stand, clad in the brown
habits that they wore in life, and labelled with
their names and the dates of their decease. Their
skulls (some quite bare, and others still covered
with yellow skin, and hair that has known the
earth-damps) look out from beneath their hoods,
grinning hideously repulsive. One reverend

father has his mouth wide open, as if he had
died in the midst of a howl of terror and remorse,
which perhaps is even now screeching through
eternity. As a general thing, however, these
frocked and hooded skeletons seem to take, a
more cheerful view of their position, and try
with ghastly smiles to turn it into a jest. But
the cemetery of the Capuchins is no place to
nourish celestial hope; the soul sinks forlorn
and wretched under all this burden of dusty
death; the holy earth from Jerusalem, so imbued
as it with mortality, has grown as barren of the
flowers of Paradise as it is of earthly weeds and
grass. Thank Heaven for its blue sky; it needs
a long, upward gaze to give us back our faith.
Not here can we feel ourselves immortal, where
the very altars in these chapels of horrible con-
secration are heaps of human bones.

Yet let us give the cemetery the praise that it
deserves. There is no disagreeable scent, such
as might have been expected from the decay of
so many holy persons, in whatever odour of

sanctity they may have taken their departure.
The same number of living monks would not
smell half so unexceptionably.

Miriam went gloomily along the corridor, from
one vaulted Golgotha to another, until in the far-
thest recess she beheld an open grave.

"Is that for him who lies yonder in the nave?"
she asked.

"Yes, signorina, this is to be the resting-place
of brother Antonio, who came to his death last
night," answered the sacristan; "and in yonder
niche, you see, sits a brother who was buried
thirty years ago, and has risen to give him
place."

"It is not a satisfactory idea," observed Miriam,
"that you poor friars cannot call even your graves
permanently your own. You must lie down in
them, methinks, with a nervous anticipation of
being disturbed, like weary men who know that
they shall be summoned out of bed at mid-
night. Is it not possible (if money were to be
paid for the privilege) to leave brother Antonio

—if that be his name—in the occupancy of that
narrow grave till the last trumpet sounds?"

"By no means, signorina; neither is it needful
or desirable," answered the sacristan. "A quarter
of a century's sleep in the sweet earth of Jeru-
salem is better than a thousand years in any other
soil. Our brethren find good rest there. No
ghost was ever known to steal out of this blessed
cemetery."

"That is well," responded Miriam; "may he
whom you now lay to sleep prove no exception
to the rule!"

As they left the cemetery she put money into
the sacristan's hand, to an amount that made his
eyes open wide and glisten, and requested that
it might be expended in masses for the repose
of Father Antonio's soul.

CHAPTER VI.

THE MEDICI GARDENS.

"DONATELLO," said Miriam, anxiously, as they came through the Piazza Barberini, "what can I do for you, my beloved friend? You are shaking as with the cold fit of the Roman fever."

"Yes," said Donatello, "my heart shivers."

As soon as she could collect her thoughts, Miriam led the young man to the gardens of the Villa Medici, hoping that the quiet shade and sunshine of that delightful retreat would a little revive his spirits. The grounds are there laid out in the old fashion of straight paths, with borders of box, which form hedges of great height and density, and are shorn and trimmed to the evenness of a wall of stone, at the top and sides. There are green alleys, with long vistas, over-

shadowed by ilex-trees; and at each intersection of
the paths, the visitor finds seats of lichen-covered
stone to repose upon, and marble statues that look
forlornly at him, regretful of their lost noses. In
the more open portions of the garden, before the
sculptured front of the villa, you see fountains
and flower-beds, and, in their season, a profusion
of roses, from which the genial sun of Italy
distils a fragrance, to be scattered abroad by the
no less genial breeze.

But Donatello drew no delight from these
things. He walked onward in silent apathy, and
looked at Miriam with strangely half-awakened
and bewildered eyes, when she sought to bring
his mind into sympathy with hers, and so re-
lieve his heart of the burden that lay lumpishly
upon it.

She made him sit down on a stone bench, where
two embowered alleys crossed each other; so that
they could discern the approach of any casual
intruder, a long way down the path.

"My sweet friend," she said, taking one of his

passive hands in both of hers, "what can I say
to comfort you?"

"Nothing!" replied Donatello, with sombre
reserve. "Nothing will ever comfort me."

"I accept my own misery," continued Miriam,
"my own guilt, if guilt it be—and, whether guilt
or misery, I shall know how to deal with it. But
you, dearest friend, that were the rarest creature
in all this world, and seemed a being to whom
sorrow could not cling—you, whom I half
fancied to belong to a race that had vanished
for ever, you only surviving, to show mankind
how genial and how joyous life used to be, in
some long-gone age—what had you to do with
grief or crime?"

"They came to me as to other men," said
Donatello, broodingly. "Doubtless I was born
to them."

"No, no; they came with me," replied Miriam.
"Mine is the responsibility! Alas! wherefore
was I born? Why did we ever meet? Why
did I not drive you from me, knowing—for my

heart foreboded it—that the cloud in which I walked would likewise envelop you!"

Donatello stirred uneasily, with the irritable impatience that is often combined with a mood of leaden despondency. A brown lizard with two tails—a monster often engendered by the Roman sunshine—ran across his foot, and made him start. Then he sat silent awhile, and so did Miriam, trying to dissolve her whole heart into sympathy, and lavish it all upon him, were it only for a moment's cordial.

The young man lifted his hand to his breast, and, intentionally, as Miriam's hand was within his, he lifted that along with it.

"I have a great weight here!" said he.

The fancy struck Miriam (but she drove it resolutely down) that Donatello almost imperceptibly shuddered, while, in pressing his own hand against his heart, he pressed hers there too.

"Rest your heart on me, dearest one!" she resumed. "Let me bear all its weight; I am well able to bear it; for I am a woman, and I love you! I love you, Donatello! Is there no comfort for you in this avowal? Look at me! Heretofore, you have found me pleasant to your sight. Gaze into my eyes! Gaze into my soul! Search as deeply as you may, you can never see half the tenderness and devotion that I henceforth cherish for you. All that I ask, is your acceptance of the utter self-sacrifice (but it shall be no sacrifice, to my great love) with which I seek to remedy the evil you have incurred for my sake!"

All this fervour on Miriam's part; on Donatello's, a heavy silence.

"Oh, speak to me!" she exclaimed. "Only promise me to be, by and by, a little happy!"

"Happy?" murmured Donatello. "Ah, never again! never again!"

"Never? Ah, that is a terrible word to say to me!" answered Miriam. "A terrible word to let fall upon a woman's heart, when she loves you, and is conscious of having caused your misery! If you love me, Donatello, speak it not again. And surely you did love me?"

"I did," replied Donatello, gloomily and absently.

Miriam released the young man's hand, but suffered one of her own to lie close to his, and waited a moment to see whether he would make any effort to retain it. There was much depending upon that simple experiment.

With a deep sigh—as when, sometimes, a slumberer turns over in a troubled dream—Donatello changed his position, and clasped both his hands over his forehead. The genial warmth of a Roman April kindling into May was in the atmosphere around them; but when Miriam saw that involuntary movement and heard that sigh of relief (for so she interpreted it), a shiver ran through her frame, as if the iciest wind of the Apennines were blowing over her.

"He has done himself a greater wrong than I dreamed of," thought she, with unutterable compassion. "Alas! it was a sad mistake! He

might have had a kind of bliss in the consequences
of this deed, had he been impelled to it by a love
vital enough to survive the frenzy of that terrible
moment—mighty enough to make its own law,
and justify itself against the natural remorse.
But to have perpetrated a dreadful murder (and
such was his crime, unless love, annihilating
moral distinctions, made it otherwise) on no better
warrant than a boy's idle fantasy! I pity him
from the very depths of my soul! As for my-
self, I am past my own or other's pity."

She arose from the young man's side, and stood
before him with a sad, commiserating aspect; it
was the look of a ruined soul, bewailing, in him,
a grief less than what her profounder sympathies
imposed upon herself.

"Donatello, we must part," she said, with
melancholy firmness. "Yes; leave me! Go
back to your old tower, which overlooks the green
valley you have told me of, among the Apennines.
Then, all that has passed will be recognized as but
an ugly dream. For, in dreams, the conscience

sleeps, and we often stain ourselves with guilt of which we should be incapable in our waking moments. The deed you seemed to do, last night, was no more than such a dream; there was as little substance in what you fancied yourself doing. Go, and forget it all!"

" Ah, that terrible face!" said Donatello, pressing his hands over his eyes. " Do you call that unreal?"

" Yes; for you beheld it with dreaming eyes," replied Miriam. " It was unreal; and, that you may feel it so, it is requisite that you see this face of mine no more. Once, you may have thought it beautiful; now, it has lost its charm. Yet it would still retain a miserable potency to bring back the past illusion, and, in its train, the remorse and anguish that would darken all your life. Leave me, therefore, and forget me."

" Forget you, Miriam!" said Donatello, roused somewhat from his apathy of despair. " If I could remember you, and behold you, apart from that frightful visage which stares at me over your shoulder, that were a consolation, at least, if not a joy."

"But since that visage haunts you along with mine," rejoined Miriam, glancing behind her, "we needs must part. Farewell, then! But if ever—in distress, peril, shame, poverty, or whatever anguish is most poignant, whatever burden heaviest—you should require a life to be given wholly, only to make your own a little easier, then summon me! As the case now stands between us, you have bought me dear, and find me of little worth. Fling me away, therefore! May you never need me more! But, if otherwise, a wish—almost an unuttered wish—will bring me to you!"

She stood a moment, expecting a reply. But Donatello's eyes had again fallen on the ground, and he had not, in his bewildered mind and over-burdened heart, a word to respond.

"That hour I speak of may never come," said Miriam. "So farewell—farewell for ever."

"Farewell," said Donatello.

His voice hardly made its way through the
environment of unaccustomed thoughts and emo-
tions which had settled over him like a dense
and dark cloud. Not improbably, he beheld
Miriam through so dim a medium that she
looked visionary; heard her speak only in a
thin, faint echo.

She turned from the young man, and, much
as her heart yearned towards him, she would
not profane that heavy parting by an embrace,
or even a pressure of the hand. So soon after
the semblance of such mighty love, and after
it had been the impulse to so terrible a deed,
they parted, in all outward show, as coldly
as people part whose whole mutual intercourse
has been encircled within a single hour.

And Donatello, when Miriam had departed,
stretched himself at full length on the stone
bench, and drew his hat over his eyes, as the
idle and light-hearted youths of dreamy Italy
are accustomed to do, when they lie down in
the first convenient shade, and snatch a noon-

day slumber. A stupor was upon him, which
he mistook for such drowsiness as he had known
in his innocent past life. But, by and by, he
raised himself slowly and left the garden. Some-
times poor Donatello started, as if he heard a
shriek; sometimes he shrank back, as if a face,
fearful to behold, were thrust close to his own.
In this dismal mood, bewildered with the novelty
of sin and grief, he had little left of that sin-
gular resemblance, on account of which, and
for their sport, his three friends had fantasti-
cally recognized him as the veritable Faun of
Praxiteles.

CHAPTER VII.

MIRIAM AND HILDA.

ON leaving the Medici Gardens, Miriam felt herself astray in the world; and having no special reason to seek one place more than another, she suffered chance to direct her steps as it would. Thus it happened, that, involving herself in the crookedness of Rome, she saw Hilda's tower rising before her, and was put in mind to climb up to the young girl's eyrie, and ask why she had broken her engagement at the church of the Capuchins. People often do the idlest acts of their lifetime in their heaviest and most anxious moments; so that it would have been no wonder, had Miriam been impelled only by so slight a motive of curiosity as we have indicated. But she remembered, too, and

with a quaking heart, what the sculptor had
mentioned of Hilda's retracing her steps towards
the courtyard of the Palazzo Caffarelli in quest
of Miriam herself. Had she been compelled to
choose between infamy in the eyes of the whole
world, or in Hilda's eyes alone, she would unhesi-
tatingly have accepted the former, on condition of
remaining spotless in the estimation of her white-
souled friend. This possibility, therefore, that
Hilda had witnessed the scene of the past night,
was unquestionably the cause that drew Miriam
to the tower, and made her linger and falter
as she approached it.

As she drew near, there were tokens to
which her disturbed mind gave a sinister inter-
protation. Some of her friend's airy family, the
doves, with their heads imbedded disconsolately
in their bosoms, were ~~huddled~~ in a corner of
the piazza; others had alighted on the heads,
wings, shoulders, and trumpets of the marble
angels which adorned the façade of the neigh-
bouring church; two or three had betaken them-

selves to the Virgin's shrine; and as many as
could find room were sitting on Hilda's win-
dow-sill. But all of them, so Miriam fancied,
had a look of weary expectation and disap-
pointment—no flights, no flutterings, no cooing
murmur; something that ought to have made
their day glad and bright, was evidently left
out of this day's history. And, furthermore,
Hilda's white window-curtain was closely drawn,
with only that one little aperture at the side,
which Miriam remembered noticing the night
before.

"Be quiet," said Miriam to her own heart,
pressing her hand hard upon it. "Why shouldst
thou throb now?—Hast thou not endured more
terrible things than this?"

Whatever were her apprehensions, she would
not turn back. It might be—and the solace
would be worth a world—that Hilda, knowing
nothing of the past night's calamity, would greet
her friend with a sunny smile, and so restore

her soul was frozen. But could Miriam, guilty
as she was, permit Hilda to kiss her cheek, to
clasp her hand, and thus be no longer so un-
spotted from the world as heretofore.

"I will never permit her sweet touch again,"
said Miriam, toiling up the staircase, "if I can
find strength of heart to forbid it. But, oh!
it would be so soothing in this wintry fever-fit
of my heart! There can be no harm to my
white Hilda in one parting kiss. That shall
be all!"

But, on reaching the upper landing - place,
Miriam paused, and stirred not again till she
had brought herself to an immoveable resolve.

"My lips, my hands shall never meet Hilda's
more," said she.

Meanwhile, Hilda sat listlessly in her paint-
ing-room. Had you looked into the little ad-
joining chamber, you might have seen the slight
imprint of her figure on the bed, but would
also have detected at once that the white coun-
terpane had not been turned down. The pillow

was more disturbed; she had turned her face upon it, the poor child, and bedewed it with some of those tears (among the most chill and forlorn that gush from human sorrow) which the innocent heart pours forth at its first actual discovery that sin is in the world. The young and pure are not apt to find out that miserable truth until it is brought home to them by the guiltiness of some trusted friend. They may have heard much of the evil of the world, and seem to know it, but only as an impalpable theory. In due time, some mortal, whom they reverence too highly, is commissioned by Providence to teach them this direful lesson; he perpetrates a sin; and Adam falls anew, and Paradise, heretofore in unfaded bloom, is lost again, and closed for ever, with the fiery swords gleaming at its gates.

The chair in which Hilda sat was near the portrait of Beatrice Cenci, which had not yet been taken from the easel. It is a peculiarity of this picture, that its profoundest expression

eludes a straightforward glance, and can only
be caught by side glimpses, or when the eye
falls casually upon it; even as if the painted
face had a life and consciousness of its own,
and, resolving not to betray its secret of grief
or guilt, permitted the true tokens to come
forth only when it imagined itself unseen.   No
other such magical effect has ever been wrought
by pencil.

Now, opposite the easel hung a looking-glass,
in which Beatrice's face and Hilda's were both
reflected.   In one of her weary, nerveless changes
of position, Hilda happened to throw her eyes
on the glass, and took in both these images at
one unpremeditated glance.   She fancied—nor
was it without horror—that Beatrice's expres-
sion, seen aside and vanishing in a moment,
had been depicted in her own face likewise,
and flitted from it as timorously.

"Am I, too, stained with guilt?" thought the
poor girl, hiding her face in her hands.

Not so, thank Heaven!   But, as regards

Beatrice's picture, the incident suggests a theory
which may account for its unutterable grief and
mysterious shadow of guilt, without detracting
from the purity which we love to attribute to
that ill-fated girl. Who, indeed, can look at
that mouth—with its lips half apart, as innocent
as a baby's that has been crying—and not pro-
nounce Beatrice sinless! It was the intimate
consciousness of her father's sin that threw its
shadow over her, and frightened her into a
remote and inaccessible region, where no sym-
pathy could come. It was the knowledge of
Miriam's guilt, that lent the same expression to
Hilda's face.

But Hilda nervously moved her chair, so that
the images in the glass should be no longer
visible. She now watched a speck of sunshine
that came through a shuttered window, and
crept from object to object, indicating each with
a touch of its bright finger, and then letting
them all vanish successively. In like manner,
her mind, so like sunlight in its natural cheerful-

ness, went from thought to thought, but found nothing that it could dwell upon for comfort. Never before had this young, energetic, active spirit known what it is to be despondent. It was the unreality of the world that made her so. Her dearest friend, whose heart seemed the most solid and richest of Hilda's possessions, had no existence for her any more; and in that dreary void, out of which Miriam had disappeared, the substance, the truth, the integrity of life, the motives of effort, the joy of success, had departed along with her.

It was long past noon, when a step came up the staircase. It had passed beyond the limits where there was communication with the lower regions of the palace, and was mounting the successive flights which led only to Hilda's precincts. Faint as the tread was, she heard and recognized it. It startled her into sudden life. Her first impulse was to spring to the door of the studio, and fasten it with lock and bolt. But a second thought made her feel that this

would be an unworthy cowardice, on her own
part, and also that Miriam—only yesterday her
closest friend—had a right to be told, face to
face, that thenceforth they must be for ever
strangers.

She heard Miriam pause, outside of the door.
We have already seen what was the latter's
resolve with respect to any kiss or pressure of
the hand between Hilda and herself. We know
not what became of the resolution. As Miriam
was of a highly impulsive character, it may
have vanished at the first sight of Hilda; but,
at all events, she appeared to have dressed her-
self up in a garb of sunshine, and was disclosed,
as the door swung open, in all the glow of her
remarkable beauty. The truth was, her heart
leaped convulsively towards the only refuge that
it had, or hoped. She forgot, just one instant,
all cause for holding herself aloof. Ordinarily
there was a certain reserve in Miriam's demon-
strations of affection, in consonance with the

delicacy of her friend. To-day, she opened her
arms to take Hilda in.

"Dearest, darling Hilda!" she exclaimed.
"It gives me new life to see you!"

Hilda was standing in the middle of the room.
When her friend made a step or two from the
door, she put forth her hands with an involun-
tory repellent gesture, so expressive, that Miriam
at once felt a great chasm opening itself between
them two. They might gaze at one another
from the opposite side, but without the possibility
of ever meeting more; or, at least, since the
chasm could never be bridged over, they must
tread the whole round of Eternity to meet on
the other side. There was even a terror in
the thought of their meeting again. It was as
if Hilda or Miriam were dead, and could no
longer hold intercourse without violating a
spiritual law.

Yet, in the wantonness of her despair, Miriam
made one more step towards the friend whom
she had lost.

"Do not come nearer, Miriam!" said Hilda.

Her look and tone were those of sorrowful entreaty, and yet they expressed a kind of confidence, as if the girl were conscious of a safeguard that could not be violated.

"What has happened between us, Hilda?" asked Miriam. "Are we not friends?"

"No, no!" said Hilda, shuddering.

"At least, we have been friends," continued Miriam. "I loved you dearly! I love you still! You were to me as a younger sister; yes, dearer than sisters of the same blood; for you and I were so lonely, Hilda, that the whole world pressed us together by its solitude and strangeness. Then, will you not touch my hand? Am I not the same as yesterday?"

"Alas! no, Miriam!" said Hilda.

"Yes, the same—the same for you, Hilda," rejoined her lost friend. "Were you to touch my hand, you would find it as warm to your grasp as ever. If you were sick or suffering, I would watch night and day for you. It is in

such simple offices that true affection shows it-
self; and so I speak of them. Yet now, Hilda,
your very look seems to put me beyond the limits
of humankind!"

"It is not I, Miriam," said Hilda; "not I
that have done this."

"You, and you only, Hilda," replied Miriam,
stirred up to make her own cause good, by
the repellent force which her friend opposed to
her. "I am a woman, as I was yesterday;
endowed with the same truth of nature, the
same warmth of heart, the same genuine and
earnest love, which you have always known in
me. In any regard that concerns yourself, I
am not changed. And believe me, Hilda, when
a human being has chosen a friend out of all
the world, it is only some faithlessness between
themselves, rendering true intercourse impossi-
ble, that can justify either friend in sever-
ing the bond. Have I deceived you? Then
cast me off! Have I wronged you personally?
Then forgive me, if you can. But, have I

sinned against God and man, and deeply sinned?
Then be more my friend than ever, for I need
you more.”

"Do not bewilder me thus, Miriam!" ex-
claimed Hilda, who had not forborne to express,
by look and gesture, the anguish which this
interview inflicted on her. "If I were one of
God's angels, with a nature incapable of stain,
and garments that never could be spotted, I
would keep ever at your side, and try to lead
you upward. But I am a poor, lonely girl,
whom God has set here in an evil world, and
given her only a white robe, and bid her wear
it back to Him, as white as when she put it on.
Your powerful magnetism would be too much
for me. The pure, white atmosphere, in which
I try to discern what things are good and true,
would be discoloured. And, therefore, Miriam,
before it is too late, I mean to put faith in this
awful heart-quake, which warns me henceforth
to avoid you."

"Ah, this is hard! Ah, this is terrible!"

murmured Miriam, dropping her forehead in her hands. In a moment or two she looked up again, as pale as death, but with a composed countenance; "I always said, Hilda, that you were merciless; for I had a perception of it, even while you loved me best. You have no sin, nor any conception of what it is; and therefore you are so terribly severe! As an angel, you are not amiss; but, as a human creature, and a woman among earthly men and women, you need a sin to soften you."

"God forgive me," said Hilda, "if I have said a needlessly cruel word!"

"Let it pass," answered Miriam; "I, whose heart it has smitten upon, forgive you. And tell me, before we part for ever, what have you seen or known of me, since we last met?"

"A terrible thing, Miriam," said Hilda, grow-ing paler than before.

"Do you see it written in my face, or painted in my eyes?" inquired Miriam, her trouble

seeking relief in a half-frenzied raillery. "I
would fain know how it is that Providence, or.
fate, brings eye-witnesses to watch us, when
we fancy ourselves acting in the remotest pri-
vacy. Did all Rome see it, then? Or, at
least, our merry company of artists? Or is it
some blood-stain on me, or death-scent in my
garments? They say that monstrous deformi-
ties sprout out of fiends, who once were lovely
angels. Do you perceive such in me already?
Tell me, by our past friendship, Hilda, all you
know."

Thus adjured, and frightened by the wild
emotion which Miriam could not suppress, Hilda
strove to tell what she had witnessed.

"After the rest of the party had passed on,
I went back to speak to you," she said; "for
there seemed to be a trouble on your mind,
and I wished to share it with you, if you could
permit me. The door of the little courtyard
was partly shut; but I pushed it open, and saw
you within, and Donatello,_and a third person,

whom I had before noticed in the shadow of a
niche. He approached you, Miriam. You knelt
to him! I saw Donatello spring upon him!
I would have shrieked, but my throat was dry;
I would have rushed forward; but my limbs
seemed rooted to the earth.—It was all like a
flash of lightning. A look passed from your
eyes to Donatello's—a look——"

"Yes, Hilda, yes!" exclaimed Miriam, with
intense eagerness. "Do not pause now! That
look?"

"It revealed all your heart, Miriam," con-
tinued Hilda, covering her eyes as if to shut
out the recollection; "a look of hatred, triumph,
vengeance, and, as it were, joy at some un-
hoped-for relief."

"Ah! Donatello was right, then," murmured
Miriam, who shook throughout all her frame.
"My eyes bade him do it! Go on, Hilda."

"It all passed so quickly—all like a glare
of lightning," said Hilda, "and yet it seemed
to me that Donatello had paused, while one

might draw a breath. But that look!—Ah, Miriam, spare me. Need I tell more?"

"No more; there needs no more, Hilda," replied Miriam, bowing her head, as if listening to a sentence of condemnation from a supreme tribunal. "It is enough! You have satisfied my mind on a point where it was greatly disturbed. Henceforward, I shall be quiet. Thank you, Hilda."

She was on the point of departing, but turned back again from the threshold.

"This is a terrible secret to be kept in a young girl's bosom," she observed; "what will you do with it, my poor child?"

"Heaven help and guide me," answered Hilda, bursting into tears; "for the burden of it crushes me to the earth! It seems a crime to know of such a thing, and to keep it to myself. It knocks within my heart continually, threatening, imploring, insisting to be let out! Oh, my mother! my mother! Were she yet living, I would travel over land and sea to tell

her this dark secret, as I told all the little
troubles of my infancy. But I am alone—
alone! Miriam, you were my dearest, only
friend. Advise me what to do."

This was a singular appeal, no doubt, from
the stainless maiden to the guilty woman, whom
she had just banished from her heart for ever.
But it bore striking testimony to the impres-
sion which Miriam's natural uprightness and
impulsive generosity had made on the friend
who knew her best; and it deeply comforted
the poor criminal, by proving to her that the
bond between Hilda and herself was vital
yet.

As far as she was able, Miriam at once re-
sponded to the girl's cry for help.

"If I deemed it good for your peace of mind,"
she said, " to bear testimony against me for
this deed, in the face of all the world, no con-
sideration of myself should weigh with me an
instant. But I believe that you would find no
relief in such a course. What men call justice

lies chiefly in outward formalities, and has never
the close application and fitness that would be
satisfactory to a soul like yours. I cannot be
fairly tried and judged before an earthly tribu-
nal; and of this, Hilda, you would perhaps
become fatally conscious, when it was too late.
Roman justice, above all things, is a byword.
What have you to do with it? Leave all such
thoughts aside! Yet, Hilda, I would not have
you keep my secret imprisoned in your heart,
if it tries to leap out, and stings you, like a
wild, venomous thing, when you thrust it back
again. Have you no other friend, now that
you have been forced to give me up?"

"No other," answered Hilda, sadly.

"Yes; Kenyon!" rejoined Miriam.

"He cannot be my friend," said Hilda, "be-
cause—because—I have fancied that he sought
to be something more."

"Fear nothing!" replied Miriam, shaking
her head, with a strange smile. "This story
will frighten his new-born love out of its little

life, if that be what you wish. Tell him the
secret, then, and take his wise and honourable
counsel as to. what should next be done. I
know not what else to say."

"I never dreamed," said Hilda,—"how could
you think it?—of betraying you to justice. But
I see how it is, Miriam. I must keep your
secret, and die of it, unless God sends me some
relief by methods which are now beyond my
power to imagine. It is very dreadful. Ah!
now I understand how the sins of generations
past have created an atmosphere of sin for
those that follow. While there is a single
guilty person in the universe, each innocent
one must feel his innocence tortured by that
guilt. Your deed, Miriam, has. darkened the
whole sky!"

Poor Hilda turned from her unhappy friend,
and, sinking on her knees in a corner of the
chamber, could not be prevailed upon to utter
another word. And Miriam, with a long regard
from the threshold, bade farewell to this doves'

nest, this one little nook of pure thoughts and innocent enthusiasms, into which she had brought such trouble. Every crime destroys more Edens than our own!

CHAPTER VIII.

THE TOWER AMONG THE APENNINES.

IT was in June, that the sculptor, Kenyon, arrived on horseback at the gate of an ancient country-house (which, from some of. its features, might almost be called a castle) situated in a part of Tuscany somewhat remote from the ordinary track of tourists. Thither we must now accompany him, and endeavour to make our story flow onward, like a streamlet, past a gray tower that rises on the hillside, overlooking a spacious valley, which is set in the grand framework of the Apennines.

The sculptor had left Rome with the retreating tide of foreign residents. For, as summer approaches, the Niobe of Nations is made to bewail anew, and doubtless with sincerity, the loss of that large part of her population, which she derives from other lands, and on whom depends much of whatever remnant of prosperity she still enjoys. Rome, at this season, is pervaded and overhung with atmospheric terrors, and insulated within a charmed and deadly circle. The crowd of wandering tourists betake themselves to Switzerland, to the Rhine, or, from this central home of the world, to their native homes in England or America, which they are apt thenceforward to look upon as provincial, after once having yielded to the spell of the Eternal City. The artist, who contemplates an indefinite succession of winters in this home of art (though his first thought was merely to improve himself by a brief visit) goes forth, in the summer time, to sketch scenery and costume among the Tuscan hills, and pour, if he can, the purple air of Italy over his canvas. He studies the old schools of art in the mountain towns where they were born, and where they are still to be seen in the faded frescoes of Giotto

and Cimabue, on the walls of many a church, or
in the dark chapels, in which the sacristan
draws aside the veil from a treasured picture of
Perugino. Thence, the happy painter goes to
walk the long, bright galleries of Florence, or
to steal glowing colours from the miraculous
works, which he finds in a score of Vene-
tian palaces. Such summers as these, spent
amid whatever is exquisite in art, or wild and
picturesque in nature, may not inadequately
repay him for the chill neglect and disappoint-
ment through which he has probably languished,
in his Roman winter. This sunny, shadowy,
breezy, wandering life, in which he seeks for
beauty as his treasure, and gathers for his
winter's honey what is but a passing fragrance
to all other men, is worth living for, come after-
wards what may. Even if he die unrecognized, the
artist has had his share of enjoyment and success.

Kenyon had seen, at a distance of many miles,
the old villa or castle towards which his journey
lay, looking from its height over a broad expanse

of valley. As he drew nearer, however, it had
been hidden among the inequalities of the hill-
side, until the winding road brought him almost
to the iron gateway. The sculptor found this
substantial barrier fastened with lock and bolt.
There was no bell, nor other instrument of
sound; and, after summoning the invisible
garrison with his voice, instead of a trumpet, he
had leisure to take a glance at the exterior of
the fortress.

About thirty yards within the gateway rose
a square tower, lofty enough to be a very
prominent object in the landscape, and more
than sufficiently massive in proportion to its
height. Its antiquity was evidently such, that,
in a climate of more abundant moisture, the ivy
would have mantled it from head to foot in a
garment that might, by this time, have been
centuries old, though ever new. In the dry
Italian air, however, Nature had only so far
adopted this old pile of stonework as to cover
almost every hand's-breadth of it with close-

26—2

clinging lichens and yellow moss; and the im-
memorial growth of these kindly productions
rendered the general hue of the tower soft and
venerable, and took away the aspect of nakedness
which would have made its age drearier than now.

Up and down the height of the tower were
scattered three or four windows, the lower ones
grated with iron bars, the upper ones vacant
both of window-frames and glass. Besides these
larger openings, there were several loopholes
and little square apertures, which might be
supposed to light the staircase, that doubtless
climbed the interior towards the battlemented
and machicolated summit. With this last-men-
tioned warlike garniture upon its stern old head
and brow, the tower seemed evidently a strong-
hold of times long past. Many a crossbowman
had shot his shafts from those windows and
loopholes, and from the vantage height of those
gray battlements; many a flight of arrows, too,
had hit all round about the embrasures above,
or the apertures below, where the helmet of a

defender had momentarily glimmered. On
festal nights, moreover, a hundred lamps had
often gleamed afar over the valley, suspended
from the iron hooks that were ranged for the
purpose beneath the battlements and every win-
dow.

Connected with the tower, and extending be-
hind it, there seemed to be a very spacious
residence, chiefly of more modern date. It per-
haps owed much of its fresher appearance, how-
ever, to a coat of stucco and yellow wash,
which is a sort of renovation very much in
vogue with the Italians. Kenyon noticed over
a doorway, in the portion of the edifice imme-
diately adjacent to the tower, a cross, which,
with a bell suspended above the roof, indicated
that this was a consecrated precinct, and the
chapel of the mansion.

Meanwhile, the hot sun so incommoded the
unsheltered traveller, that he shouted forth an-
other impatient summons. Happening, at the
same moment, to look upward, he saw a figure

leaning from an embrasure of the battlements, and gazing down at him.

"Ho, Signor Count!" cried the sculptor, waving his straw hat, for he recognized the face, after a moment's doubt. "This is a warm reception, truly! Pray bid your porter let me in, before the sun shrivels me quite into a cinder."

"I will come myself," responded Donatello, flinging down his voice out of the clouds, as it were; "old Thomaso and old Stella are both asleep, no doubt, and the rest of the people are in the vineyard. But I have expected you, and you are welcome!"

The young count—as perhaps we had better designate him in his ancestral tower—vanished from the battlements; and Kenyon saw his figure appear successively at each of the windows, as he descended. On every reappearance, he turned his face towards the sculptor and gave a nod and smile; for a kindly impulse prompted him thus to assure his visitor of a

welcome, after keeping him so long at an in-
hospitable threshold.

Kenyon, however (naturally and profession-
ally expert at reading the expression of the human
countenance) had a vague sense that this was
not the young friend whom he had known so
familiarly in Rome; not the sylvan and un-
tutored youth, whom Miriam, Hilda, and him-
self, had liked, laughed at, and sported with;
not the Donatello whose identity they had so
playfully mixed up with that of the Faun of
Praxiteles.

Finally, when his host had emerged from a
side-portal of the mansion, and approached the
gateway, the traveller still felt that there was
something lost, or something gained (he hardly
knew which) that set the Donatello of to-day
irreconcileably at odds with him of yesterday.
His very gait showed it, in a certain gravity, a
weight and measure of step, that had nothing
in common with the irregular buoyancy which
used to distinguish him. His face was paler

and thinner, and the lips less full, and less
apart.

"I have looked for you a long while," said
Donatello ; and, though his voice sounded dif-
ferently, and cut out its words more sharply
than had been its wont, still there was a smile
shining on his face, that, for the moment, quite
brought back the Faun. "I shall be more
cheerful, perhaps, now that you have come. It
is very solitary here."

"I have come slowly along, often lingering,
often turning aside," replied Kenyon ; "for I
found a great deal to interest me in the medie-
val sculpture hidden away in the churches here-
abouts. An artist, whether painter or sculptor,
may be pardoned for loitering through such a
region. But what a fine old tower! Its tall
front is like a page of black-letter, taken from
the history of the Italian republics."

"I know little or nothing of its history," said
the count, glancing upward at the battlements,
where he had just been standing. "But I

thank my forefathers for building it so high. I like the windy summit better than the world below, and spend much of my time there, now-a-days."

"It is a pity you are not a star-gazer," observed Kenyon, also looking up. "It is higher than Galileo's tower, which I saw, a week or two ago, outside of the walls of Florence."

"A star-gazer? I am one," replied Donatello. "I sleep in the tower, and often watch very late on the battlements. There is a dismal old staircase to climb, however, before reaching the top, and a succession of dismal chambers, from story to story. Some of them were prison chambers in times past, as old Tomaso will tell you."

The repugnance intimated in his tone, at the idea of this gloomy staircase and these ghostly, dimly lighted rooms, reminded Kenyon of the original Donatello, much more than his present custom of midnight vigils on the battlements.

"I shall be glad to share your watch," said the guest; "especially by moonlight. The pro-

spect of this broad valley must be very fine.
But I was not aware, my friend, that these were
your country babits. I have fancied you in a
sort of Arcadian life, tasting rich figs, and
squeezing the juice out of the sunniest grapes,
and sleeping soundly, all night, after a day of
simple pleasures."

"I may have known such a life, when I was
younger," answered the count, gravely. "I am
not a boy now. Time flies over us, but leaves
its shadow behind."

The sculptor could not but smile at the
triteness of the remark, which, nevertheless had
a kind of originality as coming from Donatello.
He had thought it out from his own experience,
and perhaps considered himself as communicating
a new truth to mankind.

They were now advancing up the courtyard;
and the long extent of the villa, with its iron-
barred lower windows and balconied upper ones,
became visible, stretching back towards a grove
of trees.

"At some period of your family history,"
observed Kenyon, "the Counts of Monte Beni
must have led a patriarchal life in this vast house.
A great-grandsire and all his descendants might
find ample verge here, and with space, too, for
each separate brood of little ones to play within
its own precincts. Is your present household
a large one?"

"Only myself," answered Donatello, "and
Tomaso, who has been butler since my grand-
father's time, and old Stella, who goes sweeping
and dusting about the chambers, and Girolamo,
the cook, who has but an idle life of it. He
shall send you up a chicken forthwith. But,
first of all, I must summon one of the contadini
from the farmhouse yonder, to take your horse
to the stable."

Accordingly, the young count shouted amain,
and with such effect, that, after several repeti-
tions of the outcry, an old gray woman protruded
her head and a broom-handle from a chamber
window; the venerable butler emerged from a

recess in the side of the house, where was a well, or reservoir, in which he had been cleansing a small wine-cask; and a sun-burnt contadino, in his shirt-sleeves, showed himself on the outskirts of the vineyard, with some kind of a farming tool in his hand. Donatello found employment for all these retainers in providing accommodation for his guest and steed, and then ushered the sculptor into the vestibule of the house.

It was a square and lofty entrance room, which, by the solidity of its construction, might have been an Etruscan tomb, being paved and walled with heavy blocks of stone, and vaulted almost as massively overhead. On two sides, there were doors. opening into long suites of ante-rooms and saloons; on the third side, a stone staircase, of spacious breadth, ascending, by dignified degrees and with wide resting-places, to another floor of similar extent. Through one of the doors, which was ajar, Kenyon beheld an almost interminable vista of apartments, opening one beyond the other, and reminding him of the hundred rooms in Blue Beard's castle, or the countless halls in some palace of the Arabian Nights.

It must have been a numerous family, indeed, that could ever have sufficed to people with human life so large an abode as this, and impart social warmth to such a wide world within doors. The sculptor confessed to himself, that Donatello could allege reason enough for growing melancholy, having only his own personality to vivify it all.

"How a woman's face would brighten it up!" he ejaculated, not intending to be overheard.

But, glancing at Donatello, he saw a stern and sorrowful look in his eyes, which altered his youthful face as much as if it had seen thirty years of trouble; and, at the same moment, old Stella showed herself through one of the doorways, as the only representative of her sex at Monte Beni.

CHAPTER IX.

SUNSHINE.

"COME," said the count, "I see you already find the old house dismal. So do I, indeed! And yet it was a cheerful place in my boyhood. But, you see, in my father's days (and the same was true of all my endless line of grandfathers, as I have heard), there used to be uncles, aunts, and all manner of kindred, dwelling together as one family. They were a merry and kindly race of people, for the most part, and kept one another's hearts warm."

"Two hearts might be enough for warmth," observed the sculptor, "even in so large a house as this. One solitary heart, it is true, may be apt to shiver a little. But, I trust, my friend, that the genial blood of your race still flows in many veins besides your own?"

"I am the last," said Donatello, gloomily. "They have all vanished from me, since my childhood. Old Tomaso will tell you that the air of Monte Beni is not so favourable to length of days as it used to be. But that is not the secret of the quick extinction of my kindred."

"Then you are aware of a more satisfactory reason?" suggested Kenyon.

"I thought of one, the other night, while I was gazing at the stars," answered Donatello; "but, pardon me, I do not mean to tell it. One cause, however, of the longer and healthier life of my forefathers, was, that they had many pleasant customs, and means of making themselves glad, and their guests and friends along with them. Now-a-days we have but one!"

"And what is that?" asked the sculptor.

"You shall see!" said his young host.

By this time, he had ushered the sculptor into one of the numberless saloons; and, calling for refreshment, old Stella placed a cold fowl upon the table, and quickly followed it with a savoury omelette, which Girolamo had lost no time in preparing. She also brought some cherries, plums, and apricots, and a plate full of particularly delicate figs, of last year's growth. The butler showing his white head at the door, his master beckoned to him.

"Tomaso, bring some Sunshine!" said he.

The readiest method of obeying this order, one might suppose, would have been, to fling wide the green window-blinds, and let the glow of the summer noon into the carefully shaded room. But, at Monte Beni, with provident caution against the wintry days, when there is little sunshine, and the rainy ones, when there is none, it was the hereditary custom to keep their Sunshine stored away in the cellar. Old Tomaso quickly produced some of it in a small, straw-covered flask, out of which he extracted the cork, and inserted a little cotton wool, to absorb the olive oil that kept the precious liquid from the air.

"This is a wine," observed the count, "the secret of making which has been kept in our family for centuries upon centuries; nor would it avail any man to steal the secret, unless he could also steal the vineyard, in which alone the Monte Beni grape can be produced. There is little else left me, save that patch of vines. Taste some of their juice, and tell me whether it is worthy to be called Sunshine! for that is its name."

"A glorious name, too!" cried the sculptor.

 "Taste it," said Donatello, filling his friend's glass and pouring likewise a little into his own. "But first smell its fragrance; for the wine is very lavish of it, and will scatter it all abroad."

"Ah, how exquisite!" said Kenyon. "No other wine has a bouquet like this. The flavour must be rare indeed, if it fulfil the promise of this fragrance, which is like the airy sweetness of youthful hopes, that no realities will ever satisfy!"

This invaluable liquor was of a pale golden

hue, like other of the rarest Italian wines, and,
if carelessly and irreligiously quaffed, might have
been mistaken for a very fine sort of Champagne.
It was not, however, an effervescing wine,
although its delicate piquancy produced a some-
what similar effect upon the palate. Sipping,
the guest longed to sip again; but the wine
demanded so deliberate a pause, in order to
detect the hidden peculiarities and subtle ex-
quisiteness of its flavour, that to drink it was
really more a moral than a physical enjoyment.
There was a deliciousness in it that eluded
analysis, and—like whatever else is superlatively
good—was perhaps better appreciated in the
memory than by present consciousness. One of
its most ethereal charms lay in the transitory
life of the wine's richest qualities; for, while it
required a certain leisure and delay, yet, if you
lingered too long upon the draught, it became
disenchanted both of its fragrance and its
flavour.

The lustre should not be forgotten, among

the other admirable endowments of the Monte
Beni wine; for, as it stood in Kenyon's glass, a
little circle of light glowed on the table round
about it, as if it were really so much golden
sunshine.

"I feel myself a better man for that ethereal
potation," observed the sculptor. "The finest
Orvieto, or that famous wine, the Est Est Est
of Montefiascone, is vulgar in comparison. This
is surely the wine of the Golden Age, such as
Bacchus himself first taught mankind to press
from the choicest of his grapes. My dear count,
why is it not illustrious? The pale, liquid gold,
in every such flask as that, might be solidified
into golden scudi, and would quickly make you
a millionaire!"

Tomaso, the old butler, who was standing by
the table, and enjoying the praises of the wine
quite as much as if bestowed upon himself,
made answer,—

"We have a tradition, signore," said he, "that
this rare wine of our vineyard would lose all

27—8

its wonderful qualities, if any of it were sent to market. The Counts of Monte Beni have never parted with a single flask of it for gold. At their banquets, in the olden time, they have entertained princes, cardinals, and once an emperor, and once a pope, with this delicious wine, and always, even to this day, it has been their custom to let it flow freely, when those whom they love and honour sit at the board. But the grand duke himself could not drink that wine, except it were under this very roof!"

"What you tell me, my good friend," replied Kenyon, "makes me venerate the Sunshine of Monte Beni even more abundantly than before. As I understand you, it is a sort of consecrated juice, and symbolizes the holy virtues of hospitality and social kindness?"

"Why, partly so, signore," said the old butler, with a shrewd twinkle in his eye: but, to speak out all the truth, there is another excellent reason why neither a cask nor a flask of our precious vintage should ever be sent to market. The wine, signore, is so fond of its native home, that a transportation of even a few miles turns it quite sour. And yet it is a wine that keeps well in the cellar, underneath this floor, and gathers fragrance, flavour, and brightness in its dark dungeon. That very flask of Sunshine, now, has kept itself for you, sir guest, (as a maid reserves her sweetness till her lover comes for it) ever since a merry vintage-time, when the Signor Count here was a boy!"

"You must not wait for Tomaso to end his discourse about the wine, before drinking off your glass," observed Donatello. "When once the flask is uncorked, its finest qualities lose little time in making their escape. I doubt whether your last sip will be quite so delicious as you found the first."

And, in truth, the sculptor fancied that the Sunshine became almost imperceptibly clouded, as he approached the bottom of the flask. The effect of the wine, however, was a gentle exhilaration, which did not so speedily pass away.

Being thus refreshed, Kenyon looked around
him at the antique saloon in which they sat. It
was constructed in a most ponderous style, with
a stone floor, on which heavy pilasters were
planted against the wall, supporting arches that
crossed one another in the vaulted ceiling. The
upright walls, as well as the compartments of
the roof, were completely covered with frescoes,
which doubtless had been brilliant when first
executed, and perhaps for generations after-
wards. The designs were of a festive and joyous
character, representing Arcadian scenes, where
nymphs, fauns, and satyrs, disported themselves
among mortal youths and maidens; and Pan,
and the god of wine, and he of sunshine and
music, disdained not to brighten some sylvan
merry-making with the scarcely veiled glory of
their presence. A wreath of dancing figures, in
admirable variety of shape and motion, was
festooned quite round the cornice of the room.

In its first splendour, the saloon must have
presented an aspect both gorgeous and enliven-

ing; for it invested some of the cheerfullest ideas
and emotions of which the human mind is
susceptible w.t the external reality of beautiful
form, and rich, harmonious glow and variety of
colour. But the frescoes were now very ancient.
They had been rubbed and scrubbed by old
Stella and many a predecessor, and had been
defaced in one spot, and retouched in another,
and had peeled from the wall in patches, and
had hidden some of their brightest portions
under dreary dust, till the joyousness had quite
vanished out of them all. It was often difficult
to puzzle out the design; and even where it
was more readily intelligible, the figures showed
like the ghosts of dead and buried joys—the
closer their resemblance to the happy past, the
gloomier now. For it is thus, that with only
an inconsiderable change, the gladdest objects
and existences become the saddest; hope fading
into disappointment; joy darkening into grief, and
festal splendour into funereal duskiness; and all
evolving, as their moral, a grim identity between

gay things and sorrowful ones. Only give them
a little time, and they turn out to be just
alike!

"There has been much festivity in this saloon,
if I may judge by the character of its frescoes,"
remarked Kenyon, whose spirits were still up-
held by the mild potency of the Monte Beni
wine. "Your forefathers, my dear count, must
have been joyous fellows, keeping up the vintage
merriment throughout the year. It does me
good to think of them gladdening the hearts of
men and women, with their wine of Sunshine,
even in the Iron age, as Pan and Bacchus,
whom we see yonder, did in the Golden one!"

"Yes; there have been merry times in the
banquet-hall of Monte Beni, even within my
own remembrance," replied Donatello, looking
gravely at the painted walls. "It was meant
for mirth, as you see; and when I brought my
own cheerfulness into the saloon, these frescoes
looked cheerful too. But methinks they have all
faded since I saw them last."

"It would be a good idea," said the sculptor,
falling into his companion's vein, and helping
him out with an illustration which Donatello
himself could not have put into shape, "to con-
vert this saloon into a chapel; and when the
priest tells his hearers of the instability of
earthly joys, and would show how drearily
they vanish, he may point to these pictures, that
were so joyous, and are so dismal. He could
not illustrate his theme so aptly in any other
way."

"True, indeed," answered the count, his for-
mer simplicity strangely mixing itself up with
an experience that had changed him; "and
yonder, where the minstrels used to stand, the
altar shall be placed. A sinful man might do
all the more effective penance in this old banquet-
hall."

"But I should regret to have suggested so
ungenial a transformation in your hospitable
saloon," continued Kenyon, duly noting the
change in Donatello's characteristics. "You

startle me, my friend, by so ascetic a design!
It would hardly have entered your head, when
we first met. Pray do not—if I may take the
freedom of a somewhat elder man to advise
you," added he, smiling—"pray do not, under a
notion of improvement, take upon yourself to
be sombre, thoughtful, and penitential, like all
the rest of us."

Donatello made no answer, but sat awhile,
appearing to follow with his eyes one of the
figures, which was repeated many times over in
the groups upon the walls and ceiling. It formed
the principal link of an allegory, by which (as
is often the case in such pictorial designs) the
whole series of frescoes were bound together,
but which it would be impossible, or, at least,
very wearisome, to unravel. The sculptor's eyes
took a similar direction, and soon began to trace
through the vicissitudes—once gay, now sombre
—in which the old artist had involved it, the
same individual figure. He fancied a resem-
blance in it to Donatello himself; and it put

him in mind of one of the purposes with which
he had come to Monte Beni.

" My dear count," said he, "I have a proposal
to make. You must let me employ a little of
my leisure in modelling your bust. You re-
member what a striking resemblance we all of us
—Hilda, Miriam, and I—found between your
features and those of the Faun of Praxiteles.
Then, it seemed an identity; but now that I
know your face better, the likeness is far less
apparent. Your head in marble would be a
treasure to me. Shall I have it?"

"I have a weakness which I fear I cannot
overcome," replied the count, turning away his
face. "It troubles me to be looked at stead-
fastly."

"I have observed it since we have been sit-
ting here, though never before," rejoined the
sculptor. "It is a kind of nervousness, I appre-
hend, which you caught in the Roman air, and
which grows upon you, in your solitary life. It
need be no hindrance to my taking your bust; for

I will catch the likeness and expression by side glimpses, which (if portrait painters and bust makers did but know it) always bring home richer results than a broad stare."

"You may take me if you have the power," said Donatello; but, even as he spoke, he turned away his face; "and if you can see what makes me shrink from you, you are welcome to put it in the bust. It is not my will, but my necessity, to avoid men's eyes. Only," he added, with a smile which made. Kenyon doubt whether he might not as well copy the Faun as model a new bust, "only, you know, you must not insist on my uncovering these ears of mine!"

"Nay; I never should dream of such a thing," answered the sculptor, laughing as the young count shook his clustering curls. "I could not hope to persuade you, remembering how Miriam once failed!"

Nothing is more unaccountable than the spell that often lurks in a spoken word. A thought

may be present to the mind, so distinctly that
no utterance could make it more so; and two
minds may be conscious of the same thought,
in which one or both take the profoundest inter-
est; but as long as it remains unspoken, their
familiar talk flows quietly over the hidden idea,
as a rivulet may sparkle and dimple over some-
thing sunken in its bed. But, speak the word;
and it is like bringing up a drowned body out
of the deepest pool of the rivulet, which has
been aware of the horrible secret all along, in
spite of its smiling surface.

And even so, when Kenyon chanced to make
a distinct reference to Donatello's relations with
Miriam (though the subject was already in both
their minds) a ghastly emotion rose up out of
the depths of the young count's heart. He
trembled either with anger or terror, and glared
at the sculptor with wild eyes, like a wolf that
meets you in the forest, and hesitates whether to
flee or turn to bay. But, as Kenyon still looked
calmly at him, his aspect gradually became less

disturbed, though far from resuming its former
quietude.

"You have spoken her name," said he, at
last, in an altered and tremulous tone; "tell me,
now, all that you know of her."

"I scarcely think that I have any later in-
telligence than yourself," answered Kenyon;
"Miriam left Rome at about the time of your
own departure. Within a day or two after our
last meeting at the church of the Capuchins,
I called at her studio and found it vacant.
Whither she has gone, I cannot tell."

Donatello asked no further questions.

They rose from table, and strolled together
about the premises, whiling away the afternoon
with brief intervals of unsatisfactory conversa-
tion, and many shadowy silences. The sculptor
had a perception of change in his companion—
possibly of growth and development, but cer-
tainly of change—which saddened him, because
it took away much of the simple grace that was
the best of Donatello's peculiarities.

Kenyon betook himself to repose that night in a grim, old, vaulted apartment, which, in the lapse of five or six centuries, had probably been the birth, bridal, and death chamber, of a great many generations of the Monte Beni family. He was aroused, soon after daylight, by the clamour of a tribe of beggars who had taken their stand in a little rustic lane that crept beside that portion of the villa, and were addressing their petitions to the open windows. By and by, they appeared to have received alms, and took their departure.

"Some charitable Christian has sent those vagabonds away," thought the sculptor, as he resumed his interrupted nap; "who could it be? Donatello has his own rooms in the tower; Stella, Tomaso, and the cook are a world's width off; and I fancied myself the only inhabitant in this part of the house."

In the breadth and space which so delightfully characterize an Italian villa, a dozen guests might have had each his suite of apartments

without infringing upon one another's ample pre-
cincts. But, so far as Kenyon knew, he was the
only visitor beneath Donatello's widely extended
roof.

CHAPTER X.

THE PEDIGREE OF MONTE BENI.

From the old butler, whom he found to be a
very gracious and affable personage, Kenyon soon
learned many curious particulars about the family
history and hereditary peculiarities of the Counts.
of Monte Beni. There was a pedigree, the
later portion of which⊖that is to say, for a little
more than a thousand years⊖a genealogist would
have found delight in tracing out, link by link,
and authenticating by records and documentary
evidences. It would have been as difficult,
however, to follow up the stream of Donatello's
ancestry to its dim source, as travellers have
found it to reach the mysterious fountains of
the Nile. And, far beyond the region of definite
and demonstrable fact, a romancer might have

strayed into a region of old poetry, where the
rich soil, so long uncultivated and untrodden,
had lapsed into nearly its primeval state of
wilderness. Among those antique paths, now
overgrown with tangled and riotous vegetation,
the wanderer must needs follow his own guid-
ance, and arrive nowhither at last.

The race of Monte Beni, beyond a doubt, was
one of the oldest in Italy, where families appear
to survive at least, if not to flourish on their
half-decayed roots, oftener than in England or
France. It came down in a broad track from
the Middle Ages; but, at epochs anterior to those,
it was distinctly visible in the gloom of the period
before chivalry put forth its flower; and farther
still, we are almost afraid to say it was seen,
though with a fainter and wavering course, in
the early morn of Christendom, when the Roman
Empire had hardly begun to show symptoms of
decline. At that venerable distance, the heralds
gave up the lineage in despair.

But where written record left the genealogy

of Monte Beni, tradition took it up, and carried
it without dread or shame beyond the Imperial
ages into the times of the Roman republic;
beyond those, again, into the epoch of kingly
rule. Nor even so remotely among the mossy
centuries did it pause, but strayed onward into
that gray antiquity of which there is no token
left, save its cavernous tombs, and a few bronzes,
and some quaintly wrought ornaments of gold,
and gems with mystic figures and inscriptions.
There, or thereabouts, the line was supposed to
have had its origin in the sylvan life of Etruria,
while Italy was yet guiltless of Rome.

Of course, as we regret to say, the earlier and
very much the larger portion of this respectable
descent—and the same is true of many briefer
pedigrees—must be looked upon as altogether
mythical. Still, it threw a romantic interest
around the unquestionable antiquity of the Monte
Beni family, and over that tract of their own
vines and fig-trees, beneath the shade of which
they had unquestionably dwelt for immemorial

ages. And there they had laid the foundations
of their tower, so long ago that one-half of its
height was said to be sunken under the surface,
and to hide subterranean chambers which once
were cheerful with the olden sunshine.

One story, or myth, that had mixed itself up
with their mouldy genealogy, interested the
sculptor by its wild, and perhaps grotesque, yet
not unfascinating peculiarity. He caught at it
the more eagerly, as it afforded a shadowy and
whimsical semblance of explanation for the like-
ness which he, with Miriam and Hilda, had seen,
or fancied, between Donatello and the Faun of
Praxiteles.

The Monte Beni family, as this legend averred,
drew their origin from the Pelasgic race, who
peopled Italy in times that may be called pre-
historic. It was the same noble breed of men,
of Asiatic birth, that settled in Greece; the same
happy and poetic kindred who dwelt in Arcadia,
and—whether they ever lived such life or not
—enriched the world with dreams, at least, and

fables, lovely, if unsubstantial, of a Golden Age.
In those delicious times, when deities and demi-
gods appeared familiarly on earth, mingling with
its inhabitants as friend with friend—when
nymphs, satyrs, and the whole train of classic
faith or fable, hardly took pains to hide them-
selves in the primeval woods—at that auspicious
period the lineage of Monte Beni had its rise.
Its progenitor was a being not altogether human,
yet partaking so largely of the gentlest human
qualities, as to be neither awful nor shocking
to the imagination. A sylvan creature, native
among the woods, had loved a mortal maiden,
and—perhaps by kindness, and the subtle cour-
tesies which love might teach to his simplicity,
or possibly by a ruder wooing—had won her
to his haunts. In due time, he gained her
womanly affection; and, making their bridal
bower, for aught we know, in the hollow of a
great tree, the pair spent a happy wedded life
in that ancient neighbourhood, where now stood
Donatello's tower.

From this union sprang a vigorous progeny that took its place unquestioned among human families. In that age, however, and long afterwards, it showed the ineffaceable lineaments of its wild paternity: it was a pleasant and kindly race of men, but capable of savage fierceness, and never quite restrainable within the trammels of social law. They were strong, active, genial, cheerful as the sunshine, passionate as the tornado. Their lives were rendered blissful by an unsought harmony with nature.

But, as centuries passed away, the Faun's wild blood had necessarily been attempered with constant intermixtures from the more ordinary streams of human life. It lost many of its original qualities, and served, for the most part, only to bestow an unconquerable vigour which kept the family from extinction, and enabled them to make their own part good throughout the perils and rude emergencies of their interminable descent. In the constant wars with which Italy was plagued, by the dissensions of her petty

states and republics, there was a demand for
native hardihood.

The successive members of the Monte Beni
family showed valour and policy enough, at all
events, to keep their hereditary possessions out
of the clutch of grasping neighbours, and pro-
bably differed very little from the other feudal
barons with whom they fought and feasted.
Such a degree of conformity with the manners
of the generations, through which it survived,
must have been essential to the prolonged con-
tinuance of the race.

It is well known, however, that any hereditary
peculiarity—as a supernumerary finger, or an
anomalous shape of feature, like the Austrian
lip—is wont to show itself in a family after a
very wayward fashion. It skips at its own
pleasure along the line, and, latent for half a
century or so, crops out again in a great-grand-
son. And thus, it was said, from a period beyond human
memory or record, there had ever and anon been
a descendant of the Monte Benis bearing nearly

all the characteristics that were attributed to the original founder of the race. Some traditions even went so far as to enumerate the ears, covered with a delicate fur, and shaped like a pointed leaf, among the proofs of authentic descent which were seen in these favoured individuals. We appreciate the beauty of such tokens of a nearer kindred to the great family of nature than other mortals bear; but it would be idle to ask credit for a statement which might be deemed to partake so largely of the grotesque.

But it was indisputable that, once in a century, or oftener, a son of Monte Beni gathered into himself the scattered qualities of his race, and reproduced the character that had been assigned to it from immemorial times. Beautiful, strong, brave, kindly, sincere, of honest impulses, and endowed with simple tastes and the love of homely pleasures, he was believed to possess gifts by which he could associate himself with the wild things of the forests, and with the fowls

of the air, and could feel a sympathy even with
the trees, among which it was his joy to dwell.
On the other hand, there were deficiencies both
of intellect and heart, and especially, as it seemed,
in the development of the higher portion of man's
nature. These defects were less perceptible in
early youth, but showed themselves more strongly
with advancing age, when, as the animal spirits
settled down upon a lower level, the representa-
tive of the Monte Benis was apt to become
sensual, addicted to gross pleasures, heavy, un-
sympathizing, and insulated within the narrow
limits of a surly selfishness.

A similar change, indeed, is no more than
what we constantly observe to take place in
persons who are not careful to substitute other
graces for those which they inevitably lose along
with the quick sensibility and joyous vivacity
of youth. At worst, the reigning Count of Monte
Beni, as his hair grew white, was still a jolly
old fellow over his flask of wine—the wine that
Bacchus himself was fabled to have taught his

sylvan ancestor how to express, and from what
choicest grapes, which would ripen only in a
certain divinely favoured portion of the Monte
Beni vineyard.

: The family, be it observed, were both proud
and ashamed of these legends; but whatever part
of them they might consent to incorporate into
their ancestral history, they steadily repudiated
all that referred to their one distinctive feature,
the pointed and furry ears. In a great many
years past, no sober credence had been yielded
to the mythical portion of the pedigree. It
might, however, be considered as typifying some
such assemblage of qualities—in this case, chiefly
remarkable for their simplicity and naturalness
—as, when they reappear in successive genera-
tions, constitute what we call family character.
The sculptor found, moreover, on the evidence
of some old portraits, that the physical features
of the race had long been similar to what he
now saw them in Donatello. With accumu-
lating years, it is true, the Monte Beni· face

had a tendency to look grim and savage; and,
in two or three instances, the family pictures
glared at the spectator in the eyes like some
surly animal, that had lost its good humour
when it outlived its playfulness.

The young count accorded his guest full
liberty to investigate the personal annals of these
pictured worthies, as well as all the rest of his
progenitors; and ample materials were at hand
in many chests of worm-eaten papers and yellow
parchments, that had been gathering into larger
and dustier piles ever since the dark ages. But,
to confess the truth, the information afforded
by these musty documents was so much more
prosaic than what Kenyon acquired from To-
maso's legends, that even the superior authen-
ticity of the former could not reconcile him to
its dulness.

What especially delighted the sculptor was
the analogy between Donatello's character, as
he himself knew it, and those peculiar traits
which the old butler's narrative assumed to have

been long hereditary in the race. He was amused at finding, too, that not only Tomaso but the peasantry of the estate and neighbouring village recognized his friend as a genuine Monte Beni, of the original type. They seemed to cherish a great affection for the young count, and were full of stories about his sportive childhood; how he had played among the little rustics, and been at once the wildest and the sweetest of them all; and how, in his very infancy, he had plunged into the deep pools of the streamlets and never been drowned, and had clambered to the topmost branches of tall trees without ever breaking his neck. No such mischance could happen to the sylvan child, because, handling all the elements of nature so fearlessly and freely, nothing had either the power or the will to do him harm.

He grew up, said these humble friends, the playmate not only of all mortal kind, but of creatures of the woods; although, when Kenyon pressed them for some particulars of this latter

mode of companionship, they could remember
little more than a few anecdotes of a pet fox,
which used to growl and snap at everybody save
Donatello himself.

But they enlarged—and never were weary of
the theme—upon the blithesome effects of Dona-
tello's presence in his rosy childhood and bud-
ding youth. Their hovels had always glowed
like sunshine when he entered them; so that,
as the peasants expressed it, their young mas-
ter had never darkened a doorway in his life.
He was the soul of vintage festivals. While
he was a mere infant, scarcely able to run
alone, it had been the custom to make him
tread the wine-press with his tender little feet,
if it were only to crush one cluster of the
grapes. And the grape-juice that gushed be-
neath his childish tread, be it ever so small in
quantity, sufficed to impart a pleasant flavour to
a whole cask of wine. The race of Monte
Beni—so these rustic chroniclers assured the
sculptor—had possessed the gift from the oldest

of old times of expressing good wine from ordi-
nary grapes, and a ravishing liquor from the choice
growth of their vineyard.

In a word, as he listened to such tales as
these, Kenyon could have imagined that the
valleys and hill-sides about him were a veri-
table Arcadia, and that Donatello was not merely
a sylvan faun, but the genial wine-god in his
very person. Making many allowances for the
poetic fancies of Italian peasants, he set it down
for fact, that his friend, in a simple way, and
among rustic folks, had been an exceedingly de-
lightful fellow in his younger days.

But the contadini sometimes added, shaking
their heads and sighing, that the young count
was sadly changed since he went to Rome.
The village girls now missed the merry smile
with which he used to greet them.

The sculptor inquired of his good friend
Tomaso, whether he, too, had noticed the sha-
dow which was said to have recently fallen over
Donatello's life.

"Ah, yes, signor!" answered the old butler,
"it is even so, since he came back from that
wicked and miserable city. The world has
grown either too evil, or else too wise and sad,
for such men as the old Counts of Monte Beni
used to be. His very first taste of it, as you
see, has changed and spoilt my poor young
lord. There had not been a single count in the
family these hundred years and more, who was
so true a Monte Beni, of the antique stamp, as
this poor signorino; and now it brings the
tears into my eyes to hear him sighing over
a cup of Sunshine! Ah, it is a sad world
now!"

"Then you think there was a merrier world
once?" asked Kenyon.

"Surely, signor," said Tomaso; "a merrier
world, and merrier Counts of Monte Beni to live
in it! Such tales of them as I have heard,
when I was a child on my grandfather's knee!
The good old man remembered a lord of Monte
Beni—at least, he had heard of such a one,

though I will not make oath upon the holy
crucifix that my grandsire lived in his time—
who used to go into the woods and call pretty
damsels out of the fountains, and out of the
trunks of the old trees. That merry lord was
known to dance with them a whole long summer
afternoon! When shall we see such frolics in
our days?"

"Not soon, I am afraid," acquiesced the
sculptor. "You are right, excellent Tomaso;
the world is sadder now!"

And, in truth, while our friend smiled at
these wild fables, he sighed in the same breath
to think how the once genial earth produces, in
every successive generation, fewer flowers than
used to gladden the preceding ones. Not that
the modes and seeming possibilities of human
enjoyment are rarer in our refined and softened
era—on the contrary, they never before were
nearly so abundant—but that mankind are get-
ting so far beyond the childhood of their race
that they scorn to be happy any longer. A

simple and joyous character can find no place
for itself among the sage and sombre figures
that would put his unsophisticated cheerfulness
to shame. The entire system of man's affairs,
as at present established, is built up purposely
to exclude the careless and happy soul. The
very children would upbraid the wretched in-
dividual who should endeavour to take life and
the world as what we might naturally suppose
them meant for—a place and opportunity for
enjoyment.

It is the iron rule in our day to require an
object and a purpose in life. It makes us all
parts of a complicated scheme of progress, which
can only result in our arrival at a colder and
drearier region than we were born in. It insists
upon everybody's adding somewhat—a mite, per-
haps, but earned by incessant effort—to an accu-
mulated pile of usefulness, of which the only
use will be, to burden our posterity with even
heavier thoughts and more inordinate labour than
our own. No life now wanders like an un-

fettered stream; there is a mill-wheel for the
tiniest rivulet to turn. We go all wrong, by too
strenuous a resolution to go all right.

Therefore it was so, at least, the sculptor (
thought, although partly suspicious of Donatello's
darker misfortune that the young count found)
it impossible now-a-days to be what his fore-
fathers had been. He could not live their
healthy life of animal spirits, in their sympathy
with nature, and brotherhood with all that
breathed around them. Nature, in beast, fowl,
and tree, and earth, flood, and sky, is what it
was of old; but sin, care, and self-consciousness
have set the human portion of the world askew;
and thus the simplest character is ever the soonest
to go astray.

"At any rate, Tomaso," said Kenyon, doing
his best to comfort the old man, "let us hope
that your young lord will still enjoy himself at
vintage-time. By the aspect of the vineyard, I
judge that this will be a famous year for the
golden wine of Monte Beni. As long as your

grapes produce that admirable liquor, sad as you think the world, neither the count nor his guests will quite forget to smile."

"Ah, signor," rejoined the butler with a sigh, "but he scarcely wets his lips with the sunny juice."

"There is yet another hope," observed Kenyon; "the young count may fall in love, and bring home a fair and laughing wife to chase the gloom out of yonder old, frescoed saloon. Do you think he could do a better thing, my good Tomaso?"

"Maybe not, signor," said the sage butler, looking earnestly at him; "and, maybe, not a worse!"

The sculptor fancied that the good old man had it partly in his mind to make some remark, or communicate some fact, which, on second thoughts, he resolved to keep concealed in his own breast. He now took his departure cellarward, shaking his white head and muttering to himself, and did not reappear till dinner-time,

when he favoured Kenyon, whom he had taken (-
far into his good graces, with a choicer flask of)
Sunshine than had yet blessed his palate.

To say the truth, this golden wine was no
unnecessary ingredient towards making the life
of Monte Beni palatable. It seemed a pity that
Donatello did not drink a little more of it, and
go jollily to bed at least, even if he should
awake with an accession of darker melancholy
the next morning.

Nevertheless, there was no lack of outward
means for leading an agreeable life in the old
villa. Wandering musicians haunted the pre-
cincts of Monte Beni, where they seemed to
claim a prescriptive right; they made the lawn
and shrubbery tuneful with the sound of fiddle,
harp, and flute, and now and then with the
tangled squeaking of a bagpipe. Improvisatori
likewise came and told tales or recited verses
to the contadini—among whom Kenyon often (
was an auditor—after their day's work in the).
vineyard. Jugglers, too, obtained permission to

do feats of magic in the hall, where they set
even the sage Tomaso, and Stella, Girolamo,
and the peasant girls from the farmhouse, all
of a broad grin, between merriment and wonder.
These good people got food and lodging for
their pleasant pains, and some of the small wine
of Tuscany, and a reasonable handful of the
Grand Duke's copper coin, to keep up the
hospitable renown of Monte Beni. But very
seldom had they the young count as a listener,
or a spectator.

There were sometimes dances by moonlight
on the lawn, but never since he came from
Rome did Donatello's presence deepen the
blushes of the pretty contadinas, or his footstep
weary out the most agile partner or competitor,
as once it was sure to do.

Paupers—for this kind of vermin infested the
house of Monte Beni worse than any other
spot in beggar-haunted Italy—stood beneath all
the windows, making loud supplication, or even
establishing themselves on the marble steps of

the grand entrance. They ate and drank, and filled their bags, and pocketed the little money that was given them, and went forth on their devious ways, showering blessings innumerable on the mansion and its lord, and on the souls of his deceased forefathers, who had always been just such simpletons as to be compassionate to beggary. But, in spite of their favourable prayers—by which Italian philanthropists set great store—a cloud seemed to hang over these once Arcadian precincts, and to be darkest around the summit of the tower where Donatello was wont to sit and-brood.

CHAPTER XL

MYTHS.

AFTER the sculptor's arrival, however, the young count sometimes came down from his forlorn elevation, and rambled with him among the neighbouring woods and hills. He led his friend to many enchanting nooks, with which he himself had been familiar in his childhood. But of late, as he remarked to Kenyon, a sort of strangeness had overgrown them, like clusters of dark shrubbery, so that he hardly recognized the places which he had known and loved so well.

To the sculptor's eye, nevertheless, they were still rich with beauty. They were picturesque in that sweetly impressive way, where wildness, in a long lapse of years, has crept over scenes

that have been once adorned with the careful
art and toil of man; and when man could do
no more for them, time and nature came, and
wrought hand in hand to bring them to a soft
and venerable perfection. There grew the fig-
tree that had run wild, and taken to wife the
vine, which likewise had gone rampant out of
all human control; so that the two wild things
had tangled and knotted themselves into a wild
marriage-bond, and hung their various progeny
—the luscious figs, the grapes, oozy with the
southern juice, and both endowed with a wild
flavour that added the final charm—on the same
bough together.

In Kenyon's opinion, never was any other
nook so lovely as a certain little dell which he
and Donatello visited. It was hollowed in among
the hills, and open to a glimpse of the broad,
fertile valley. A fountain had its birth here,
and fell into a marble basin, which was all
covered with moss and shaggy with water-weeds.
Over the gush of the small stream, with an urn

in her arms, stood a marble nymph, whose
nakedness the moss had kindly clothed as with
a garment; and the long trails and tresses of
the maiden-hair had done what they could in
the poor thing's behalf, by hanging themselves
about her waist. In former days—it might be
a remote antiquity—this lady of the fountain
had first received the infant tide into her urn,
and poured it thence into the marble basin. But
now the sculptured urn had a great crack from
top to bottom; and the discontented nymph was
compelled to see the basin fill itself through a
channel which she could not control, although
with water long ago consecrated to her.

For this reason, or some other, she looked
terribly forlorn; and you might have fancied
that the whole fountain was but the overflow of
her lonely tears.

"This was a place that I used greatly to
delight in," remarked Donatello, sighing. "As
a child, and as a boy, I have been very happy
here."

"And, as a man, I should ask no fitter place
to be happy in," answered Kenyon. "But you,
my friend, are of such a social nature, that I
should hardly have thought these lonely haunts
would take your fancy. It is a place for a poet
to dream in, and people it with the beings of his
imagination."

"I am no poet, that I know of," said Dona-
tello, "but yet, as I tell you, I have been very
happy here, in the company of this fountain and
this nymph. It is said that a Faun, my oldest
forefather, brought home hither to this very spot
a human maiden, whom he loved and wedded.
This spring of delicious water was their household
well."

"It is a most enchanting fable!" exclaimed
Kenyon; "that is, if it be not a fact."

"And why not a fact?" said the simple
Donatello. "There is likewise another sweet
old story connected with this spot. But, now
that I remember it, it seems to me more sad
than sweet, though formerly the sorrow, in

which it closes, did not so much impress me.
If I had the gift of tale-telling, this one would
be sure to interest you mightily."

"Pray tell it," said Kenyon; "no matter
whether well or ill. These wild legends have
often the most powerful charm when least art-
fully told."

So the young count narrated a myth of one
of his progenitors—he might have lived a cen-
tury ago, or a thousand years, or before the
Christian epoch, for anything that Donatello
knew to the contrary—who had made acquain-
tance with a fair creature belonging to this
fountain. Whether woman or sprite was a mys-
tory, as was all else about her, except that her
life and soul were somehow interfused through-
out the gushing water. She was a fresh, cool,
dewy thing, sunny and shadowy, full of pleasant
little mischiefs, fitful and changeable with the
whim of the moment, but yet as constant as
her native stream, which kept the same gush
and flow for ever, while marble crumbled over

and around it. The fountain woman loved the youth—a knight, as Donatello called him—for, according to the legend, his race was akin to hers. At least, whether kin or no, there had been friendship and sympathy of old betwixt an ancestor of his, with furry ears, and the long-lived lady of the fountain. And, after all those ages, she was still as young as a May-morning, and as frolicksome as a bird upon a tree, or a breeze that makes merry with the leaves.

She taught him how to call her from her pebbly source, and they spent many a happy hour together, more especially in the fervour of the summer days. For often as he sat waiting for her by the margin of the spring, she would suddenly fall down around him in a shower of sunny rain-drops, with a rainbow glancing through them, and forthwith gather herself up into the likeness of a beautiful girl, laughing—or was it the warble of the rill over the pebbles?—to see the youth's amazement.

no 41

Thus, kind maiden that she was, the hot
atmosphere became deliciously cool and fragrant
for this favoured knight; and, furthermore, when
he knelt down to drink out of the spring,
nothing was more common than for a pair of
rosy lips to come up out of its little depths,
and touch his mouth with the thrill of a sweet,
cool, dewy kiss!

"It is a delightful story for the hot noon of
your Tuscan summer," observed the sculptor,
at this point. "But the deportment of the
watery lady must have had a most chilling in-
fluence in mid-winter. Her lover would find it,
very literally, a cold reception!"

"I suppose," said Donatello, rather sulkily,
"you are making fun of the story. But I see
nothing laughable in the thing itself, nor in what
you say about it."

He went on to relate, that for a long while,
the knight found infinite pleasure and comfort in
the friendship of the fountain nymph. In his
merriest hours, she gladdened him with her

sportive humour. If ever he was annoyed with earthly trouble, she laid her moist hand upon his brow, and charmed the fret and fever quite away.

But one day—one fatal noontide—the young knight came rushing with hasty and irregular steps to the accustomed fountain. He called the nymph: but—no doubt because there was something unusual and frightful in his tone—she did not appear, nor answer him. He flung himself down, and washed his hands and bathed his feverish brow in the cool, pure water. And then, there was a sound of woe; it might have been a woman's voice; it might have been only the sighing of the brook over the pebbles. The water shrank away from the youth's hands, and left his brow as dry and feverish as before.

Donatello here came to a dead pause.

"Why did the water shrink from this unhappy knight?" inquired the sculptor.

"Because he had tried to wash off a blood-stain!" said the young count, in a horror-stricken whisper. "The guilty man had polluted the pure water. The nymph might have comforted him in sorrow, but could not cleanse his conscience of a crime."

"And did he never behold her more?" asked Kenyon.

"Never but once," replied his friend. "He never beheld her blessed face but once again; and then there was a blood-stain on the poor nymph's brow; it was the stain his guilt had left in the fountain where he tried to wash it off. He mourned for her his whole life long, and employed the best sculptor of the time to carve this statue of the nymph from his description of her aspect. But, though my ancestor would fain have had the image wear her happiest look, the artist, unlike yourself, was so impressed with the mournfulness of the story, that, in spite of his best efforts, he made her forlorn, and for ever weeping, as you see!"

Kenyon found a certain charm in this simple

legend. Whether so intended or not, he under-
stood it as an apologue, typifying the soothing
and genial effects of an habitual intercourse with
nature, in all ordinary cares and griefs; while,
on the other hand, her mild influences fall short
in their effect upon the ruder passions, and are
altogether powerless in the dread fever-fit or
deadly chill of guilt.

"Do you say," he asked, "that the nymph's
face has never since been shown to any mortal?
Methinks, you, by your native qualities, are as
well entitled to her favour as ever your pro-
genitor could have been. Why have you not
summoned her?"

"I called her often when I was a silly child,"
answered Donatello; and he added, in an inward
voice,—" Thank Heaven, she did not come!"

"Then you never saw her?" said the sculp-
tor.

"Never in my life!" rejoined the count,
" No, my dear friend, I have not seen the nymph;
although here, by her fountain, I used to make

many strange acquaintances; for, from my earliest
childhood, I was familiar with whatever creatures
haunt the woods. You would have laughed to
see the friends I had among them; yes, among
the wild, nimble things, that reckon man their
deadliest enemy! How it was first taught me,
I cannot tell; but there was a charm—a voice,
a murmur, a kind of chaunt—by which I called
the woodland inhabitants, the furry people, and
the feathered people, in a language that they
seemed to understand."

"I have heard of such a gift," responded the
sculptor gravely, "but never before met with a
person endowed with it. Pray, try the charm;
and lest I should frighten your friends away,
I will withdraw into this thicket, and merely
peep at them."

"I doubt," said Donatello, "whether they
will remember my voice now. It changes, you
know, as the boy grows towards manhood."

Nevertheless, as the young count's good na-
ture and easy persuasibility were among his best

characteristics, he set about complying with Ken-
yon's request. The latter, in his concealment
among the shrubberies, heard him send forth
a sort of modulated breath, wild, rude, yet har-
monious. It struck the auditor as at once the
strangest and the most natural utterance that
had ever reached his ears. Any idle boy, it
should seem, singing to himself, and setting his
wordless song to no other or more definite tune
than the play of his own pulses, might produce
a sound almost identical with this; and yet, it
was as individual as a murmur of the breeze.
Donatello tried it, over and over again, with
many breaks, at first, and pauses of uncertainty;
then with more confidence, and a fuller swell,
like a wayfarer groping out of. obscurity into
the light, and moving with freer footsteps as it
brightens around him.

Anon, his voice appeared to fill the air, yet
not with an obtrusive clangour. The sound was
of a murmurous character, soft, attractive, per-
suasive, friendly. The sculptor fancied that such

might have been the original voice and utterance
of the natural man, before. the sophistication
of the human intellect formed what we now call
language. In this broad dialect—broad as the
sympathies of nature—the human brother might
have spoken to his inarticulate brotherhood that
prowl the woods, or soar upon the wing, and
have been intelligible, to such extent as to win
their confidence.

The sound had its pathos too. At some of
its simple cadences, the tears came quietly into
Kenyon's eyes. They welled up slowly from
his heart, which was thrilling with an emotion
more delightful than he had often felt before,
but which he forbore to analyze, lest, if he seized
it, it should at once perish in his grasp.

Donatello paused two or three times, and
seemed to listen; then recommencing, he poured
his spirit and life more earnestly into the strain.
And, finally—or else the sculptor's hope and
imagination deceived him — soft treads were
audible upon the fallen leaves. There was a

30—2

rustling among the shrubbery; a whirl of wings, moreover, that hovered in the air. It may have been all an illusion; but Kenyon fancied that he could distinguish the stealthy, cat-like movement of some small forest citizen, and that he could even see its doubtful shadow, if not really its substance. But, all at once, whatever might be the reason, there ensued a hurried rush and scamper of little feet; and then the sculptor heard a wild, sorrowful cry, and through the crevices of the thicket beheld Donatello fling himself on the ground.

Emerging from his hiding-place, he saw no living thing, save a brown lizard (it was of the tarantula species) rustling away through the sunshine. To all present appearance, this venomous reptile was the only creature that had responded to the young count's efforts to renew his intercourse with the lower orders of nature.

"What has happened to you?" exclaimed Kenyon, stooping down over his friend, and wondering at the anguish which he betrayed.

"Death, death!" sobbed Donatello. "They know it!"

He grovelled beside the fountain, in a fit of such passionate sobbing and weeping, that it seemed as if his heart had broken, and spilt its wild sorrows upon the ground. His unrestrained grief and childish tears made Kenyon sensible in how small a degree the customs and restraints of society had really acted upon this young man, in spite of the quietude of his ordinary deportment. In response to his friend's efforts to console him, he murmured words hardly more articulate than the strange chaunt which he had so recently been breathing into the air.

"They know it!" was all that Kenyon could yet distinguish. "They know it!"

"Who know it?" asked the sculptor. "And what is it they know?"

"They know it!" repeated Donatello, trembling. "They shun me! All nature shrinks from me, and shudders at me! I live in the midst of a curse, that hems me round with a circle of fire! No innocent thing can come near me."

"Be comforted, my dear friend," said Kenyon, kneeling beside him. "You labour under some illusion, but no curse. As for this strange, natural spell, which you have been exercising, and of which I have heard before, though I never believed in, nor expected to witness it, I am satisfied that you still possess it. It was my own half-concealed presence, no doubt, and some involuntary little movement of mine, that scared away your forest friends."

"They are friends of mine no longer," answered Donatello.

"We all of us, as we grow older," rejoined Kenyon, "lose somewhat of our proximity to nature. It is the price we pay for experience."

"A heavy price, then!" said Donatello, rising from the ground. "But we will speak no more of it. Forget this scene, my dear friend. In your eyes, it must look very absurd. It is a grief, I presume, to all men, to find the pleasant

privileges and properties of early life departing
from them. That grief has now befallen me.
Well; I shall waste no more tears for such a
cause!"

Nothing else made Kenyon so sensible of a
change in Donatello, as his newly acquired power
of dealing with his own emotions, and, after a
struggle more or less fierce, thrusting them down
into the prison-cells where he usually kept them
confined. The restraint which he now put upon
himself, and the mask of dull composure which
he succeeded in clasping over his still beautiful
and once faun-like face, affected the sensitive
sculptor more sadly than even the unrestrained
passion of the preceding scene. It is a very
miserable epoch, when the evil necessities of life,
in our tortuous world, first get the better of us
so far, as to compel us to attempt throwing a
cloud over our transparency. Simplicity in-
creases in value the longer we can keep it, and
the farther we carry it onward into life; the
loss of a child's simplicity, in the inevitable lapse

of years, causes but a natural sigh or two, because even his mother feared that he could not keep it always. But after a young man has brought it through his childhood, and has still worn it in his bosom, not as an early dew-drop, but as a diamond of pure, white lustre,— it is a pity to lose it, then. And thus, when Kenyon saw how much his friend had now to hide, and how well he hid it, he could have wept, although his tears would have been even idler than those which Donatello had just shed.

They parted on the lawn before the house, the count to climb his tower, and the sculptor to read an antique edition of Dante, which he had found among some old volumes of Catholic devotion, in a seldom-visited room. Tomaso met him in the entrance hall, and showed a desire to speak.

"Our poor signorino looks very sad to-day!" he said.

"Even so, good Tomaso," replied the sculptor. "Would that we could raise his spirits a little!"

"There might be means, signor," answered

the old butler, "if one might but be sure that
they were the right ones. We men are but
rough nurses for a sick body or a sick spirit."

"Women, you would say, my good friend, are
better," said the sculptor, struck by an intelli-
gence in the butler's face. "That is possible!
But it depends."

"Ah; we will wait a little longer," said
Tomaso, with the customary shake of his head.

CHAPTER XII.

THE OWL TOWER.

"WILL you not show me your tower?" said the sculptor one day to his friend.

"It is plainly enough to be seen, methinks," answered the count, with a kind of sulkiness that often appeared in him, as one of the little symptoms of inward trouble.

"Yes; its exterior is visible far and wide," said Kenyon. "But such a gray, moss-grown tower as this, however valuable as an object of scenery, will certainly be quite as interesting inside as out. It cannot be less than six hundred years old; the foundations and lower story are much older than that, I should judge; and traditions probably cling to the walls within quite as plentifully as the gray and yellow lichens cluster on its face without."

"No doubt," replied Donatello, "but I know little of such things, and never could comprehend the interest which some of you Forestieri take in them. A year or two ago an English signor with a venerable white beard—they say he was a magician, too—came hither from as far off as Florence, just to see my tower."

"Ah, I have seen him at Florence," observed Kenyon. "He is a necromancer, as you say, and dwells in an old mansion of the Knights Templars, close by the Ponte Vecchio, with a great many ghostly books, pictures, and antiquities, to make the house gloomy, and one bright-eyed little girl to keep it cheerful!"

"I know him only by his white beard," said Donatello; "but he could have told you a great deal about the tower, and the sieges which it has stood, and the prisoners who have been confined in it. And he gathered up all the traditions of the Monte Beni family, and, among the rest, the sad one which I told you at the fountain, the other day. He had known mighty poets, he said,

in his earlier life; and the most illustrious of
them would have rejoiced to preserve such a
legend in immortal rhyme—especially if he could
have had some of our wine of Sunshine to help
out his inspiration!"

"Any man might be a poet, as well as
Byron, with such wine and such a theme," re-
joined the sculptor. "But, shall we climb your
tower? The thunder-storm gathering yonder
among the hills will be a spectacle worth wit-
nessing."

"Come, then," said the count, adding with a
sigh, "it has a weary staircase, and dismal
chambers, and it is very lonesome at the
summit!"

"Like a man's life, when he has climbed to
eminence," remarked the sculptor; "or, let us
rather say, with its difficult steps, and the dark
prison cells you speak of, your tower resembles
the spiritual experience of many a sinful soul,
which, nevertheless, may struggle upward into the
pure air and light of heaven at last!"

Donatello sighed again, and led the way up
into the tower.

Mounting the broad staircase that ascended
from the entrance hall, they traversed the great
wilderness of a house, through some obscure
passages, and came to a low, ancient doorway.
It admitted them to a narrow turret-stair which
zigzagged upward, lighted in its progress by
loopholes and iron-barred windows. Reaching
the top of the first flight, the count threw open
a door of worm-eaten oak, and disclosed a cham-
ber that occupied the whole area of the tower.
It was most pitiably forlorn of aspect, with a
brick-paved floor, bare holes through the massive
walls, grated with iron, instead of windows, and
for furniture an old stool, which increased the
dreariness of the place tenfold, by suggesting an
idea of its having once been tenanted.

" This was a prisoner's cell in the old days,"
said Donatello; " the white-bearded necromancer,
of whom I told you, found out that a certain
famous monk was confined here, about five hun-

dred years ago. He was a very holy man, and
was afterwards burned at the stake in the Grand-
ducal Square at Firenze. There have always
been stories, Tomaso says, of a hooded monk
creeping up and down these stairs, or standing
in the doorway of this chamber. It must needs
be the ghost of the ancient prisoner. Do you
believe in ghosts?

"I can hardly tell," replied Kenyon, "on the
whole, I think not."

"Neither do I," responded the count; "for,
if spirits ever come back, I should surely have
met one within these two months past. Ghosts
never rise! So much I know, and am glad to
know it!"

Following the narrow staircase still higher,
they came to another room of similar size and
equally forlorn, but inhabited by two personages
of a race which from time immemorial have held
proprietorship and occupancy in ruined towers.
These were a pair of owls, who, being doubtless
acquainted with Donatello, showed little sign of

alarm at the entrance of visitors. They gave a dismal croak or two, and hopped aside into the darkest corner; since it was not yet their hour to flap duskily abroad.

"They do not desert me, like my other feathered acquaintances," observed the young count, with a sad smile, alluding to the scene which Kenyon had witnessed at the fountain-side. "When I was a wild, playful boy, the owls did not love me half so well."

He made no further pause here, but led his friend up another flight of steps; while, at every stage, the windows and narrow loopholes afforded Kenyon more extensive eye-shots over hill and valley, and allowed him to taste the cool purity of the mid atmosphere. At length they reached the topmost chamber, directly beneath the roof of the tower.

"This is my own abode," said Donatello; "my own owl's nest."

In fact, the room was fitted up as a bed-chamber, though in a style of the utmost simplicity. It likewise served as an oratory; there being a crucifix in one corner, and a multitude of holy emblems, such as Catholics judge it necessary to help their devotion withal. Several ugly little prints, representing the sufferings of the Saviour, and the martyrdoms of saints, hung on the wall; and, behind the crucifix, there was a good copy of Titian's Magdalen of the Pitti Palace, clad only in the flow of her golden ringlets. She had a confident look (but it was Titian's fault, not the penitent woman's) as if expecting to win heaven by the free display of her earthly charms. Inside of a glass case appeared an image of the sacred Bambino, in the guise of a little waxen boy, very prettily made, reclining among flowers, like a Cupid, and holding up a heart that resembled a bit of red sealing-wax. A small vase of precious marble was full of holy water.

Beneath the crucifix, on a table, lay a human skull, which looked as if it might have been dug up out of some old grave. But, examining

it more closely, Kenyon saw that it was carved
in gray alabaster, most skilfully done to the
death, with accurate imitation of the teeth, the
sutures, the empty eye-caverns, and the fragile
little bones of the nose. This hideous emblem
rested on a cushion of white marble, so nicely
wrought that you seemed to see the impression
of the heavy skull in a silken and downy sub-
stance.

Donatello dipped his fingers into the holy-water
vase, and crossed himself. After doing so, he
trembled.

"I have no right to make the sacred symbol
on a sinful breast!" he said.

"On what mortal breast can it be made then?"
asked the sculptor. "Is there one that hides no
sin?"

"But these blessed emblems make you smile,
I fear," resumed the count, looking askance at
his friend. "You heretics, I know, attempt to
pray without even a crucifix to kneel at."

"I, at least, whom you call a heretic, re-

verence that holy symbol," answered Kenyon.
"What I am most inclined to murmur at, is
this death's head. I could laugh, moreover, in
its ugly face! It is absurdly monstrous, my
dear friend, thus to fling the dead weight of
our mortality upon our immortal hopes. While
we live on earth, 'tis true we must needs carry
our skeletons about with us; but, for Heaven's
sake, do not let us burden our spirits with them,
in our feeble efforts to soar upward! Believe
me, it will change the whole aspect of death, if
you can once disconnect it, in your idea, with
that corruption from which it disengages our
higher part."

"I do not well understand you," said Dona-
tello; and he took up the alabaster skull, shudder-
ing, and evidently feeling it a kind of penance
to touch it. "I only know that this skull has
been in my family for centuries. Old Tomaso
has a story that it was copied by a famous
sculptor from the skull of that same unhappy
knight who loved the fountain-lady, and lost

her by a blood-stain. He lived and died with a deep sense of sin upon him, and, on his death-bed, he ordained that this token of him should go down to his posterity. And my forefathers, being a cheerful race of men in their natural disposition, found it needful to have the skull often before their eyes, because they dearly loved life and its enjoyments, and hated the very thought of death."

"I am afraid," said Kenyon, "they liked it none the better, for seeing its face under this abominab'e mask."

Without further discussion, the count led the way up one more flight of stairs, at the end of which they emerged upon the summit of the tower. The sculptor felt as if his being were suddenly magnified a hundredfold; so wide was the Umbrian valley that suddenly opened before him, set in its grand framework of nearer and more distant hills. It seemed as if all Italy lay under his eyes in that one picture. For there was the broad, sunny. smile of God, which we

31—2

fancy to be spread over that favoured land more
abundantly than on other regions, and, beneath
it, glowed a most rich and varied fertility. The
trim vineyards were there, and the fig-trees, and
the mulberries, and the smoky-bued tracts of the
olive-orchards; there, too, were fields of every
kind of grain, among which waved the Indian
corn, putting Kenyon in mind of the fondly
remembered acres of his father's homestead.
White villas, gray convents, church-spires, vil-
lages, towns, each with its battlemented walls
and towered gateway, were scattered upon this
spacious map; a river gleamed across it; and
lakes opened their blue eyes in its face, reflecting
heaven, lest mortals should forget that better
land, when they beheld the earth so beau-
tiful.

What made the valley look still wider, was
the two or three varieties of weather that were
visible on its surface, all at the same instant
of time. Here lay the quiet sunshine; there
fell the great black patches of ominous shadow

from the clouds; and behind them, like a giant
of league-long strides, came hurrying the thun-
der-storm, which had already swept midway
across the plain. In the rear of the approach-
ing tempest, brightened forth again the sunny
splendour, which its progress had darkened
with so terrible a frown.

All round this majestic landscape, the bald-
peaked or forest-crowned mountains descended
boldly upon the plain. On many of their spurs
and midway declivities, and even on their sum-
mits, stood cities, some of them famous of old;
for these had been the seats and nurseries of
early Art, where the flower of Beauty sprang
out of a rocky soil, and in a high, keen at-
mosphere, when the richest and most sheltered
gardens failed to nourish it.

"Thank God for letting me again behold
this scene!" said the sculptor, a devout man in
his way, reverently taking off his hat. " I
have viewed it from many points, and never
without as full a sensation of gratitude as my

heart seems capable of feeling. How it strengthens
the poor human spirit in its reliance on His
providence, to ascend but this little way above
the common level, and so attain a somewhat
wider glimpse of His dealings with mankind!
He doeth all things right! His will be done!"

"You discern something that is hidden from
me," observed Donatello, gloomily, yet striving
with unwonted grasp to catch the analogies
which so cheered his friend. "I see sunshine
on one spot, and cloud in another, and no reason
for it in either case. The sun on you; the
cloud on me! What comfort can I draw from
this?"

"Nay; I cannot preach," said Kenyon, "with
a page of heaven and a page of earth spread
wide open before us! . Only begin to read it,
and you will find it interpreting itself without
the aid of words. It is a great mistake to try
to put our best thoughts into human language.
When we ascend into the higher regions of
emotion and spiritual enjoyment, they are only

expressible by such grand hieroglyphics as these
around us."

They stood awhile, contemplating the scene;
but, as inevitably happens after a spiritual flight,
it was not long before the sculptor. felt his
wings flagging in the rarity of the upper at-
mosphere. He was glad to let himself quietly
downward out of the mid-sky, as it were, and
alight on the solid platform of the battlemented
tower. He looked about him, and beheld grow-
ing out of the stone pavement, which formed
the roof, a little shrub, with green and glossy
leaves. It was the only green thing there;
and heaven knows how its seeds had ever been
planted, at that airy height, or how it had
found nourishment for its small life, in the
chinks of the stones; for it had no earth, and
nothing more like soil than the crumbling mortar,
which had been crammed into the crevices in a
long-past age.

Yet the plant seemed fond of its native site;
and Donatello said it had always grown there,

from his earliest remembrance, and never, he
believed, any smaller or any larger than they
saw it now.

"I wonder if the shrub teaches you any
good lesson," said he, observing the interest
with which Kenyon examined it. "If the wide
valley has a great meaning, the plant ought to
have at least a little one; and it has been grow-
ing on our tower long enough to have learned
how to speak it."

"Oh, certainly!" answered the sculptor; "the
shrub has its moral, or it would have perished
long ago. And, no doubt, it is for your use
and edification, since you have had it before
your eyes all your lifetime, and now are moved
to ask what may be its lesson."

"It teaches me nothing," said the simple
Donatello, stooping over the plant, and perplex-
ing himself with a minute scrutiny. "But here
was a worm that would have killed it; an ugly
creature, which I will fling over the battlements."

CHAPTER XIII.

ON THE BATTLEMENTS.

THE sculptor now looked through an embrasure, and threw down a bit of lime, watching its fall, till it struck upon a stone bench at the rocky foundation of the tower, and flew into many fragments.

"Pray pardon me for helping Time to crumble away your ancestral walls," said he. "But I am one of those persons who have a natural tendency to climb heights, and to stand on the verge of them, measuring the depth below. If I were to do just as I like, at this moment, I should fling myself down after that bit of lime. It is a very singular temptation, and all but irresistible; partly, I believe, because it might be so easily done, and partly because such mo-

mentous consequences would ensue, without my
being compelled to wait a moment for them.
Have you never felt this strange impulse of an
evil spirit at your back, shoving you towards a
precipice?"

"Ah, no!" cried Donatello, shrinking from
the battlemented wall with a face of horror.
"I cling to life in a way which you cannot con-
ceive; it has been so rich, so warm, so sunny!—
and beyond its verge, nothing but the chilly
dark! And then a fall from a precipice is such
an awful death!"

"Nay; if it be a great height," said Kenyon,
"a man would leave his life in the air, and
never feel the hard shock at the bottom."

"That is not the way with this kind of death!"
exclaimed Donatello, in a low, horror-stricken
voice, which grew higher and more full of emo-
tion, as he proceeded. "Imagine a fellow-crea-
ture—breathing, now, and looking you in the face
—and now tumbling down, down, down, with
a long shriek wavering after him, all the way!

He does not leave his life in the air! No; but
it keeps in him till he thumps against the stones,
a horribly long while; then, he lies there fright-
fully quiet, a dead heap of bruised flesh and
broken bones! A quiver runs through the
crushed mass; and no more movement after that!
No; not if you would give your soul to make
him stir a finger! Ah, terrible! Yes, yes; I
would fain fling myself down for the very dread
of it, that I might endure it once for all, and
dream of it no more!"

"How forcibly—how frightfully you conceive
this!" said the sculptor, aghast at the passionate
horror which was betrayed in the count's words,
and still more in his wild gestures and ghastly
look. "Nay, if the height of your tower affects
your imagination thus, you do wrong to trust
yourself here in solitude, and in the night-time,
and at all unguarded hours. You are not safe
in your chamber. It is but a step or two; and
what if a vivid dream should lead you up hither
at midnight, and act itself out as a reality!"

Donatello had hidden his face in his hands, and was leaning against the parapet.

"No fear of that!" said he. "Whatever the dream may be, I am too genuine a coward to act out my own death in it."

The paroxysm passed away, and the two friends continued their desultory talk, very much as if no such interruption had occurred. Nevertheless, it affected the sculptor with infinite pity to see this young man, who had been born to gladness as an assured heritage, now involved in a misty bewilderment of grievous thoughts, amid which he seemed to go staggering blindfold. Kenyon, not without an unshaped suspicion of the definite fact, knew that his condition must have resulted from the weight and gloom of life, now first, through the agency of a secret trouble, making themselves felt on a character that had heretofore breathed only an atmosphere of joy. The effect of this hard lesson upon Donatello's intellect and disposition was very striking. It was perceptible that he had already had glimpses of strange and

subtile matters in those dark caverns, into which
all men must descend, if they would know any-
thing beneath the surface and illusive pleasures
of existence. And when they emerge, though
dazzled and blinded by the first glare of daylight,
they take truer and sadder views of life for ever
afterwards.

From some mysterious source, as the sculptor
felt assured, a soul had been inspired into the
young count's simplicity, since their intercourse
in Rome. He now showed a far deeper sense,
and an intelligence that began to deal with
high subjects, though in a feeble and childish
way. He evinced, too, a more definite and
nobler individuality, but developed out of grief
and pain, and fearfully conscious of the pangs
that had given it birth. Every human life, if
it ascends to truth or delves down to reality,
must undergo a similar change; but sometimes,
perhaps, the instruction comes without the sor-
row; and oftener the sorrow teaches no lesson
that abides with us. In Donatello's case, it

prepared he stood, on this old battle-field of the world, to fight with such an inevitable foe as mortal calamity, and sin for its stronger ally.

"And yet," thought Kenyon, "the poor fellow bears himself like a hero, too! If he would only tell me his trouble, or give me an opening to speak frankly about it, I might help him; but he finds it too horrible to be uttered, and fancies himself the only mortal that ever felt the anguish of remorse. Yes; he believes that nobody ever endured his agony before; so that—sharp enough in itself—it has all the additional zest of a torture just invented to plague him individually."

The sculptor endeavoured to dismiss the painful subject from his mind; and, leaning against the battlements, he turned his face southward and westward, and gazed across the breadth of

the valley. His thoughts flew far beyond even
those wide boundaries, taking an air-line from
Donatello's tower to another turret that ascended
into the sky of the summer afternoon, invisibly
to him, above the roofs of distant Rome. Then
rose tumultuously into his consciousness that
strong love for Hilda, which it was his habit to
confine in one of the heart's inner chambers, be-
cause he had found no encouragement to bring
it forward. But now, he felt a strange pull at
his heart-strings. It could not have been more
perceptible, if all the way between these battle-
ments and Hilda's dovecote had stretched an ex-
quisitely sensitive cord, which, at the hither end,
was knotted with his aforesaid heart - strings
and at the remoter one, was grasped by a
gentle hand. His breath grew tremulous. He
put his hand to his breast; so distinctly did he
seem to feel that cord drawn once and again,
and again, as if—though still it was bashfully
intimated—there were an importunate demand
for his presence. Oh! for the white wings of

Hilda's doves, that he might have flown thither, and alighted at the Virgin's shrine!

But lovers, and Kenyon knew it well, project so lifelike a copy of their mistresses out of their own imaginations, that it can pull at the heart-strings almost as perceptibly as the genuine original. No airy intimations are to be trusted; no evidences of responsive affection less positive than whispered and broken words, or tender pressures of the hand, allowed and half re- turned; or glances, that distil many passionate avowals into one gleam of richly coloured light. Even these should be weighed rigorously, at the instant; for, in another instant, the imagina- tion seizes on them as its property, and stamps them with its own arbitrary value. But Hilda's maidenly reserve had given her lover no such tokens, to be interpreted either by his hopes or fears.

"Yonder, over mountain and valley, lies Rome," said the sculptor; "shall you return thither in the autumn?"

"Never! I hate Rome," answered Donatello, "and have good cause."

"And yet it was a pleasant winter. that we spent there," observed Kenyon, "and with pleasant friends about us. You would meet them again there—all of them."

"All?" asked Donatello.

"All, to the best of my belief," said the sculptor; "but you need not go to Rome to seek them. If there were one of those friends whose life-line was twisted with your own, I. am enough of a fatalist to feel assured that you will meet that one again, wander whither you may. Neither can we escape the companions whom Providence assigns for us, by climbing an old tower like this."

"Yet the stairs are steep and dark," rejoined the count; "none but yourself would seek me here, or find me, if they sought."

As Donatello did not take advantage of this opening which his friend had kindly afforded him to pour out his hidden troubles, the latter

again threw aside the subject, and returned to
the enjoyment of the scene before him. The
thunder-storm, which he had beheld striding
across the valley, had passed to the left of Monte
Beni, and was continuing its march towards the
hills that formed the boundary on the eastward.
Above the whole valley, indeed, the sky was
heavy with tumbling vapours, interspersed with
which were tracts of blue, vividly brightened
by the sun; but in the east, where the tempest
was yet trailing its ragged skirts, lay a dusky
region of cloud and sullen mist, in which some
of the hills appeared of a dark purple hue.
Others became so indistinct, that the spectator
could not tell rocky height from impalpable
cloud. Far into this misty cloud-region, how-
ever—within the domain of chaos, as it were—
hill-tops were seen brightening in the sunshine;
they looked like fragments of the world, broken
adrift and based on nothingness, or like portions
of a sphere destined to exist, but not yet finally
compacted.

The sculptor, habitually drawing many of the images and illustrations of his thoughts from the plastic art, fancied that the scene represented the process of the Creator, when He held the new, imperfect earth in His hand, and modelled it.

"What a magic is in mist and vapour among the mountains!" he exclaimed. "With their help, one single scene becomes a thousand. The cloud-scenery gives such variety to a hilly landscape that it would be worth while to journalize its aspect from hour to hour. A cloud, however, as I have myself experienced, is apt to grow solid and as heavy as a stone the instant that you take in hand to describe it. But, in my own art, I have found great use in clouds. Such silvery ones as those to the northward, for example, have often suggested sculpturesque groups, figures, and attitudes; they are especially rich in attitudes of living repose, which a sculptor only hits upon by the rarest good fortune. When I go back to my dear native land, the clouds along the horizon will be my only gallery of art!"

"I can see cloud-shapes too," said Donatello; "yonder is one that shifts strangely; it has been like people whom I knew. And now, if I watch it a little longer, it will take the figure of a monk reclining, with his cowl about his head and drawn partly over his face, and—well! did I not tell you so?"

"I think," remarked Kenyon, "we can hardly be gazing at the same cloud. What I behold is a reclining figure, to be sure, but feminine, and with a despondent air, wonderfully well expressed in the wavering outline from head to foot. It moves my very heart by something indefinable that it suggests."

"I see the figure, and almost the face," said the count, adding, in a lower voice, "It is Miriam's!"

"No, not Miriam's," answered the sculptor.

While the two gazers thus found their own reminiscences and presentiments floating among the clouds, the day drew to its close, and now showed them the fair spectacle of an Italian sunset. The sky was soft and bright, but not

so gorgeous as Kenyon had seen it, a thousand
times, in America; for there the western sky is
wont to be set aflame with breadths and depths
of colour, with which poets seek in vain to dye
their verses, and which painters never dare to
copy. As beheld from the tower of Monte Beni,
the scene was tenderly magnificent, with mild
gradations of hue, and a lavish outpouring of
gold, but rather such gold as we see on the leaf
of a bright flower than the burnished glow of
metal from the mine. Or, if metallic, it looked
airy and unsubstantial, like the glorified dreams
of an alchemist. And speedily—more speedily
than in our own clime—came the twilight and,
brightening through its gray transparency, the
stars.

A swarm of minute insects that had been
hovering all day round the battlements were now
swept away by the freshness of a rising breeze.
The two owls in the chamber beneath Donatello's
uttered their soft, melancholy cry—which, with
national avoidance of harsh sounds, Italian owls

substitute for the hoot of their kindred in other
countries, and flew darkling forth among the
shrubbery. A convent-bell rang out, near at
hand, and was not only echoed among the hills,
but answered by another bell, and still another,
which doubtless had farther and farther re-
sponses, at various distances along the valley;
for, like the English drum-beat around the globe,
there is a chain of convent-bells from end to
end, and cross-wise, and in all possible directions,
over priest-ridden Italy.

"Come," said the sculptor, "the evening air
grows cool. It is time to descend."

"Time for you, my friend," replied the count,
and he hesitated a little before adding; "I must
keep a vigil here for some hours longer. It is
my frequent custom to keep vigils; and some-
times the thought occurs to me whether it were
not better to keep them in yonder convent, the
bell of which just now seemed to summon me.
Would I do wisely, do you think, to exchange
this old tower for a cell?"

"What! Turn monk?" exclaimed his friend.
"A horrible idea!"

"True," said Donatello, sighing. "Therefore,
if at all, I purpose doing it."

"Then think of it no more, for Heaven's
sake!" cried the sculptor. "There are a thou-
sand better and more poignant methods of being
miserable than that, if to be miserable is what
you wish. Nay; I question whether a monk
keeps himself up to the intellectual and spiritual
height which misery implies. A monk—I judge
from their sensual physiognomies, which meet
me at every turn—is inevitably a beast! Their
souls, if they have any to begin with, perish
out of them, before their sluggish, swinish
existence is half done. Better, a million times,
to stand star-gazing on these airy battlements,
than to smother your new germ of a higher life
in a monkish cell!"

"You make me tremble," said Donatello, "by
your bold aspersion of men who have devoted
themselves to God's service!"

"They serve neither God nor man, and themselves least of all, though their motives be utterly selfish," replied Kenyon. "Avoid the convent, my dear friend, as you would shun the death of the soul! But, for my own part, if I had an insupportable burden—if, for any cause, I were bent upon sacrificing every earthly hope as a peace-offering towards heaven—I would make the wide world my cell, and good deeds to mankind my prayer. Many penitent men have done this, and found peace in it."

"Ah! but you are a heretic!" said the count.

Yet his face brightened beneath the stars; and, looking at it through the twilight, the sculptor's remembrance went back to that scene in the Capitol, where, both in features and expression, Donatello had seemed identical with the Faun. And still there was a resemblance; for now, when first the idea was suggested of living for the welfare of his fellow-creatures, the original beauty, which sorrow had partly effaced, came back elevated and spiritualized.

In the black depths, the Faun had found a soul,
and was struggling with it towards the light of
heaven.

The illumination, it is true, soon faded out
of Donatello's face. The idea of life-long and
unselfish effort was too high to be received by
him with more than a momentary comprehen-
sion. An Italian, indeed, seldom dreams of
being philanthropic, except in bestowing alms
among the paupers, who appeal to his benefi-
cence at every step; nor does it occur to him
that there are fitter modes of propitiating Heaven
than by penances, pilgrimages, and offerings at
shrines. Perhaps, too, their system has its share
of moral advantages; they, at all events, cannot
well pride themselves, as our own more ener-
getic benevolence is apt to do, upon sharing
in the counsels of Providence and kindly help-
ing out its otherwise impracticable designs.

And now the broad valley twinkled with
lights, that glimmered through its duskiness,
like the fire-flies in the garden of a Florentine

palace. A gleam of lightning from the rear of
the tempest showed the circumference of hills,
and the great space between, as the last can-
non-flash of a retreating army reddens across
the field where it has fought. The sculptor
was on the point of descending the turret-
stair, when, somewhere in the darkness that lay
beneath them, a woman's voice was heard, sing-
ing a low, sad strain.

"Hark!" said he, laying his hand on Dona-
tello's arm.

And Donatello had said "Hark!" at the same
instant.

The song, if song it could be called, that
had only a wild rhythm, and flowed forth in
the fitful measure of a wind-harp, did not
clothe itself in the sharp brilliancy of the Italian
tongue. The words, so far as they could be
distinguished, were German, and therefore un-
intelligible to the count, and hardly less so to
the sculptor; being softened and molten, as it
were, into the melancholy richness of the voice

that sang them. It was as the murmur of a soul bewildered amid the sinful gloom of earth, and retaining only enough memory of a better state to make sad music of the wail, which would else have been a despairing shriek. Never was there profounder pathos than breathed through that mysterious voice; it brought the tears into the sculptor's eyes, with remembrances and forebodings of whatever sorrow he had felt or apprehended; it made Donatello sob, as chiming in with the anguish that he found unutterable, and giving it the expression which he vaguely sought.

But, when the emotion was at its profoundest depth, the voice rose out of it, yet so gradually that a gloom seemed to pervade it, far upward from the abyss, and not entirely to fall away as it ascended into a higher and purer region. At last, the auditors would have fancied that the melody, with its rich sweetness all there, and much of its sorrow gone, was floating around the very summit of the tower.

"Donatello," said the sculptor, when there was silence again, "had that voice no message for your ear?"

"I dare not receive it," said Donatello; "the anguish of which it spoke abides with me; the hope dies away with the breath that brought it hither. It is not good for me to hear that voice."

The sculptor sighed, and left the poor penitent keeping his vigil on the tower.

CHAPTER XIV.

DONATELLO'S BUST.

KENYON, it will be remembered, had asked Dona-
tello's permission to model his bust. The work
had now made considerable progress, and neces-
sarily kept the sculptor's thoughts brooding much
and often upon his host's personal characteristics.
These it was his difficult office to bring out from
their depths, and interpret them to all men, show-
ing them what they could not discern for them-
selves, yet must be compelled to recognize at a
glance, on the surface of a block of marble.

He had never undertaken a portrait-bust which
gave him so much trouble as Donatello's; not
that there was any special difficulty in hitting the
likeness, though even in this respect the grace
and harmony of the features seemed inconsistent

but he was chiefly perplexed how to make this genial and kindly type of countenance the index of the mind within. His acuteness and his sympathies, indeed, were both somewhat at fault in their efforts to enlighten him as to the moral phase through which the count was now passing. If at one sitting he caught a glimpse of what appeared to be a genuine and permanent trait, it would probably be less perceptible on a second occasion, and perhaps have vanished entirely at a third. So evanescent a show of character threw the sculptor into despair; not marble or clay, but cloud and vapour was the material in which it ought to be represented. Even the ponderous depression which constantly weighed upon Donatello's heart could not compel him into the kind of repose which the plastic art requires.

Hopeless of a good result, Kenyon gave up all preconceptions about the character of his subject, and let his hands work uncontrolled with the clay, somewhat as a spiritual medium, while holding

a pen, yields it to an unseen guidance other than
that of her own will. Now and then he fancied
that his plan was destined to be the successful
one. A skill and insight beyond his conscious-
ness seemed occasionally to take up the task.
The mystery, the miracle, of imbuing an inani-
mate substance with thought, feeling, and all the
intangible attributes of the soul, appeared on the
verge of being wrought. And now, as he flattered
himself, the true image of his friend was about
to emerge from the facile material, bringing with
it more of Donatello's character than the keenest
observer could detect at any one moment in the
face of the original. Vain expectation! some
touch, whereby the artist thought to improve or
hasten the result, interfered with the design of
his unseen spiritual assistant, and spoilt the whole.
There was still the moist, brown clay, indeed,
and the features of Donatello, but without any
semblance of intelligent and sympathetic life.

"The difficulty will drive me mad, I verily
believe!" cried the sculptor, nervously. "Look

at the wretched piece of work yourself, my dear friend, and tell me whether you recognize any manner of likeness to your inner man?"

"None," replied Donatello, speaking the simple truth. "It is like looking a stranger in the face."

This frankly unfavourable testimony so wrought with the sensitive artist, that he fell into a passion with the stubborn image, and cared not what might happen to it thenceforward. Wielding that wonderful power which sculptors possess over moist clay, however refractory it may show itself in certain respects, he compressed, elongated, widened, and otherwise altered the features of the bust in mere recklessness, and at every change inquired of the count whether the expression became anywise more satisfactory.

"Stop!" cried Donatello at last, catching the sculptor's hand. "Let it remain so!"

By some accidental handling of the clay, entirely independent of his own will, Kenyon had given the countenance a distorted and violent look combining animal fierceness with intelligent hatred. Had Hilda, or had Miriam seen the bust, with the expression which it had now assumed, they might have recognized Donatello's face as they beheld it at that terrible moment when he held his victim over the edge of the precipice.

"What have I done?" said the sculptor, shocked at his own casual production. "It were a sin to let the clay which bears your features harden into a look like that. Cain never wore an uglier one."

"For that very reason, let it remain!" answered the count, who had grown pale as ashes at the aspect of his crime, thus strangely presented to him in another of the many guises under which guilt stares the criminal in the face. "Do not alter it! Chisel it, rather, in eternal marble! I will set it up in my oratory and keep it continually before my eyes. Sadder and more horrible is a face like this, alive with my own crime, than the dead skull which my forefathers handed down to me!"

But, without in the least heeding Donatello's remonstrances, the sculptor again applied his artful fingers to the clay, and compelled the bust to dismiss the expression that had so startled them both.

"Believe me," said he, turning his eyes upon his friend, full of grave and tender sympathy; "you know not what is requisite for your spiritual growth, seeking, as you do, to keep your soul perpetually in the unwholesome region of remorse. It was needful for you to pass through that dark valley, but it is infinitely dangerous to linger there too long; there is poison in the atmosphere, when we sit down and brood in it, instead of girding up our loins to press onward. Not despondency, not slothful anguish, is what you now require—but effort! Has there been an unutterable evil in your young life? Then crowd it out with good, or it will lie corrupting there for ever, and cause your capacity for better things to partake its noisome corruption!"

"You stir up many thoughts," said Donatello,

pressing his hand upon his brow, "but the multitude and the whirl of them make me dizzy."

They now left the sculptor's temporary studio, without observing that his last accidental touches, with which he hurriedly effaced the look of deadly rage, had given the bust a higher and sweeter expression than it had hitherto worn. It is to be regretted that Kenyon had not seen it; for only an artist, perhaps, can conceive the irksomeness, the irritation of brain, the depression of spirits, that resulted from his failure to satisfy himself, after so much toil and thought as he had bestowed on Donatello's bust. In case of success, indeed, all this thoughtful toil would have been reckoned, not only as well bestowed, but as among the happiest hours of his life; whereas, deeming himself to have failed, it was just so much of life that had better never have been lived; for thus does the good or ill result of his labour throw back sunshine or gloom upon the artist's mind. The sculptor, therefore, would have done well to glance again at his work; for here were still the features of the antique Faun, but now illuminated with a higher meaning, such as the old marble never bore.

Donatello having quitted him, Kenyon spent the rest of the day strolling about the pleasant precincts of Monte Beni, where the summer was now so far advanced that it began, indeed, to partake of the ripe wealth of autumn. Apricots had long been abundant, and had passed away, and plums and cherries along with them. But now came great, juicy pears, melting and delicious, and peaches of goodly size and tempting aspect, though cold and watery to the palate, compared with the sculptor's rich reminiscences of that fruit in America. The purple figs had already enjoyed their day, and the white ones were luscious now. The contadini (who, by this time, knew Kenyon well) found many clusters of ripe grapes for him, in every little globe of which was included a fragrant draught of the sunny Monte Beni wine.

Unexpectedly, in a nook, close by the farm-

house, he chanced to find a spot where the
vintage had actually commenced. A great heap
of early ripened grapes had been gathered, and
thrown into a mighty tub. In the middle of it
stood a lusty and jolly contadino, nor stood
merely, but stamped with all his might, and
danced amain; while the red juice bathed his
feet, and threw its foam midway up his brown
and shaggy legs. Here, then, was the very
process that figures so picturesquely in Scripture
and in poetry, of treading out the wine-press
and dyeing the feet and garments with the
crimson effusion, as with the blood of a battle-
field.. The memory of the process does not make
the Tuscan wine taste more deliciously. The
contadini hospitably offered Kenyon a sample
of the new liquor, that had already stood fer-
menting for a day or two. He had tried a
similar draught, however, in years past, and
was little inclined to make proof of it again;
for he knew that it would be a sour and bitter
juice, a wine of woe and tribulation, and that,

the more a man drinks of such liquor, the sadder he is likely to be.

The scene reminded the sculptor of our New England vintages, where the big piles of golden and rosy apples lie under the orchard trees, in the mild, autumnal sunshine; and the creaking cider-mill, set in motion by a circumgyrotary horse, is all a-gush with the luscious juice. To speak frankly, the cider-making is the more picturesque sight of the two, and the new, sweet cider an infinitely better drink than the ordinary, unripe Tuscan wine. Such as it is, however, the latter fills thousands upon thousands of small, flat barrels, and, still growing thinner and sharper, loses the little life it had as wine, and becomes apotheosized as a more praiseworthy vinegar.

Yet all these vineyard scenes, and the processes connected with the culture of the grape, had a flavour of poetry about them. The toil that produces those kindly gifts of nature which are not the substance of life, but its luxury, is unlike other toil. We are inclined to fancy that

it does not bend the sturdy frame and stiffen
the overwrought muscles, like the labour that is
devoted in sad, hard earnest to raise grain for
sour bread. Certainly, the sunburnt young men
and dark-cheeked laughing girls, who weeded
the rich acres of Monte Beni, might well enough
have passed for inhabitants of an unsophisticated
Arcadia. Later in the season, when the true
vintage-time should come, and the wine of Sun-
shine gush into the vats, it was hardly too wild
a dream that Bacchus himself might revisit the
haunts which he loved of old. But, alas, where
now would he find the Faun with whom we
see him consorting in so many an antique
group?

Donatello's remorseful anguish saddened this
primitive and delightful life. Kenyon had a pain
of his own, moreover, although not all a pain,
in the never quiet, never satisfied yearning of
his heart towards Hilda. He was authorized to
use little freedom towards that shy maiden, even
in his visions; so that he almost reproached

himself when sometimes his imagination pictured
in detail the sweet years that they might spend
together, in a retreat like this. It had just that
rarest quality of remoteness from the actual and
ordinary world—a remoteness through which all
delights might visit them freely, sifted from all
troubles—which lovers so reasonably insist upon,
in their ideal arrangements for a happy union.
It is possible, indeed, that even Donatello's grief
and Kenyon's pale, sunless affection, lent a charm
to Monte Beni, which it would not have retained
amid a more redundant joyousness. The sculp-
tor strayed amid its vineyards and orchards, its
dells and tangled shrubberies, with somewhat the
sensations of an adventurer who should find his
way to the site of ancient Eden, and behold its
loveliness through the transparency of that gloom
which has been brooding over those haunts of
innocence ever since the fall. Adam saw it in
a brighter sunshine, but never knew the shade
of pensive beauty which Eden won from his ex-
pulsion.

It was in the decline of the afternoon that Kenyon returned from his long, musing ramble. Old Tomaso—between whom and himself, for some time past, there had been a mysterious understanding—met him in the entrance hall, and drew him a little aside.

"The signorina would speak with you," he whispered.

"In the chapel?" asked the sculptor.

"No; in the saloon beyond it," answered the butler; "the entrance—you once saw the signorina appear through it—is near the altar, hidden behind the tapestry."

Kenyon lost no time in obeying the summons.

CHAPTER XV.

THE MARBLE SALOON.

In an old Tuscan villa, a chapel ordinarily makes one among the numerous apartments; though it often happens that the door is permanently closed, the key lost, and the place left to itself, in dusty sanctity, like that chamber in man's heart where he hides his religious awe. This was very much the case with the chapel of Monte Beni. One rainy day, however, in his wanderings through the great, intricate house, Kenyon had unexpectedly found his way into it, and been impressed by its solemn aspect. The arched windows, high upward in the wall, and darkened with dust and cobweb, threw down a dim light that showed the altar, with a picture of a martyrdom above,

and some tall tapers ranged before it. They
had apparently been lighted, and burned an
hour or two, and been extinguished perhaps
half a century before. The marble vase at the
entrance held some hardened mud at the bottom,
accruing from the dust that had settled in it
during the gradual evaporation of the holy
water; and a spider (being an insect that de-
lights in pointing the moral of desolation and
neglect) had taken pains to weave a prodi-
giously thick tissue across the circular brim.
An old family banner, tattered by the moths,
drooped from the vaulted roof. In niches, there
were some mediæval busts of Donatello's for-
gotten ancestry; and among them, it might be,
the forlorn visage of that hapless knight be-
tween whom and the fountain-nymph had occurred
such tender love passages.

Throughout all the jovial prosperity of Monte
Beni, this one spot within the domestic walls
had kept itself silent, stern, and sad. When
the individual or the family retired from song

and mirth, they here sought those realities which men do not invite their festive associates to share. And here, on the occasion above referred to, the sculptor had discovered—accidentally, so far as he was concerned, though with a purpose on her part—that there was a guest under Donatello's roof, whose presence the count did not suspect. An interview had since taken place, and he was now summoned to another.

He crossed the chapel, in compliance with Tomaso's instructions, and, passing through the side entrance, found himself in a saloon, of no great size, but more magnificent than he had supposed the villa to contain. As it was vacant, Kenyon had leisure to pace it once or twice, and examine it with a careless sort of scrutiny, before any person appeared.

This beautiful hall was floored with rich marbles, in artistically arranged figures and compartments. The walls, likewise, were almost entirely cased in marble of various kinds, the prevalent variety being giallo antico, intermixed

with verde antique, and others equally precious.
The splendour of the giallo antico, however,
was what gave character to the saloon; and
the large and deep niches, apparently intended
for full-length statues, along the walls, were
lined with the same costly material. Without
visiting Italy, one can have no idea of the
beauty and magnificence that are produced by
these fittings-up of polished marble. Without
such experience, indeed, we do not even know
what marble means, in any sense, save as the
white limestone of which we carve our mantel-
pieces. This rich hall of Monte Beni, more-
over, was adorned, at its upper end, with two
pillars that seemed to consist of oriental ala-
baster; and wherever there was a space vacant
of precious and variegated marble, it was fres-
coed with ornaments in arabesque. Above, there
was a coved and vaulted ceiling, glowing with
pictured scenes, which affected Kenyon with a
vague sense of splendour, without his twisting
his neck to gaze at them.

It is one of the special excellences of such a saloon of polished and richly coloured marble, that decay can never tarnish it. Until the house crumbles down upon it, it shines indestructibly, and with a little dusting looks just as brilliant in its three hundredth year as the day after the final slab of giallo antico was fitted into the wall. To the sculptor, at this first view of it, it seemed a hall where the sun was magically imprisoned, and must always shine. He anticipated Miriam's entrance, arrayed in queenly robes, and beaming with even more than the singular beauty that had heretofore distinguished her.

While this thought was passing through his mind, the pillared door, at the upper end of the saloon, was partly opened, and Miriam appeared. She was very pale, and dressed in deep mourning. As she advanced towards the sculptor, the feebleness of her step was so apparent that he made haste to meet her, apprehending that she might sink down on the marble floor, without the instant support of his arm.

But, with a gleam of her natural self-reliance, she declined his aid, and, after touching her cold hand to his, went and sat down on one of the cushioned divans that were ranged against the wall.

"You are very ill, Miriam!" said Kenyon, much shocked at her appearance. "I had not thought of this."

"No; not so ill as I seem to you," she answered, adding despondently, "yet I am ill enough, I believe, to die, unless some change speedily occurs."

"What, then, is your disorder?" asked the sculptor; "and what the remedy?"

"The disorder!" repeated Miriam. "There is none that I know of, save too much life and strength, without a purpose for one or the other. It is my too redundant energy that is slowly— or perhaps rapidly—wearing me away, because I can apply it to no use. The object, which I am bound to consider my only one on earth, fails me utterly. The sacrifice which I yearn to make of myself, my hopes, my everything, is coldly put aside. Nothing is left for me but to brood, brood, brood, all day, all night, in unprofitable longings and repinings."

"This is very sad, Miriam," said Kenyon.

"Ay, indeed; I fancy so," she replied, with a short, unnatural laugh.

"With all your activity of mind," resumed he, "so fertile in plans as I have known you, can you imagine no method of bringing your resources into play?"

"My mind is not active any longer," answered Miriam, in a cold, indifferent tone. "It deals with one thought and no more. One recollection paralyzes it. It is not remorse; do not think it! I put myself out of the question, and feel neither regret nor penitence on my own behalf. But what benumbs me—what robs me of all power—it is no secret for a woman to tell a man, yet I care not though you know it—is the certainty that I am, and must ever be, an object of horror in Donatello's sight."

The sculptor—a young man, and cherishing

a love which insulated him from the wild ex-
periences which some men gather—was startled
to perceive how Miriam's rich, ill-regulated nature
impelled her to fling herself, conscience and all,
on one passion, the object of which intellectually
seemed far beneath her.

"How have you obtained the certainty of
which you speak?" asked he, after a pause.

"Oh, by a sure token," said Miriam; "a
gesture, merely; a shudder, a cold shiver that ran
through him one sunny morning when his hand
happened to touch mine! But it was enough."

"I firmly believe, Miriam," said the sculptor,
"that he loves you still."

She started, and a flush of colour came tremu-
lously over the paleness of her cheek.

"Yes," repeated Kenyon, "if my interest in
Donatello—and in yourself, Miriam—endows me
with any true insight, he not only loves you
still, but with a force and depth proportioned to
the stronger grasp of his faculties, in their new
development."

"Do not deceive me," said Miriam, growing pale again.

"Not for the world!" replied Kenyon. "Here is what I take to be the truth. There was an interval, no doubt, when the horror of some calamity, which I need not shape out in my conjectures, threw Donatello into a stupor of mystery. Connected with the first shock there was an intolerable pain and shuddering repugnance attaching themselves to all the circumstances and surroundings of the event that so terribly affected him. Was his dearest friend involved within the horror of that moment, he would shrink from her as he shrank most of all from himself. But, as his mind roused itself—as it rose to a higher life than he had hitherto experienced—whatever had been true and permanent within him revived by the selfsame impulse. So has it been with his love."

"But, surely," said Miriam, "he knows that I am here! Why, then, except that I am odious to him, does he not bid me welcome?"

"He is, I believe, aware of your presence here," answered the sculptor. "Your song, a night or two ago, must have revealed it to him; and, in truth, I had fancied that there was already a consciousness of it in his mind. But, the more passionately he longs for your society, the more religiously he deems himself bound to avoid it. The idea of a life-long penance has taken strong possession of Donatello. He gropes blindly about him for some method of sharp self-torture, and finds, of course, no other so efficacious as this."

"But he loves me," repeated Miriam, in a low voice, to herself. "Yes; he loves me!"

It was strange to observe the womanly softness that came over her, as she admitted that comfort into her bosom. The cold, unnatural indifference of her manner, a kind of frozen passionateness, which had shocked and chilled the sculptor, disappeared. She blushed, and turned away her eyes, knowing that there was more surprise and joy in their dewy glances, than any man save one ought to detect there.

34—2

"In other respects," she inquired at length, "is he much changed?"

"A wonderful process is going forward in Donatello's mind," answered the sculptor. "The germs of faculties that have heretofore slept are fast springing into activity. The world of thought is disclosing itself to his inward sight. He startles me, at times, with his perception of deep truths; and, quite as often, it must be owned, he compels me to smile by the intermixture of his former simplicity with a new intelligence. But, he is bewildered with the revelations that each day brings. Out of his bitter agony, a soul and intellect, I could almost say, have been inspired into him."

"Ah, I could help him here!" cried Miriam, clasping her hands. "And how sweet a toil to bend and adapt my whole nature to do him good! To instruct, to elevate, to enrich his mind with the wealth that would flow in upon me, had I such a motive for acquiring it! Who else can perform the task? Who else has the tender

sympathy which he requires? Who else, save
only me—a woman, a sharer in the same dread
secret, a partaker in one identical guilt—could
meet him on such terms of intimate equality as
the case demands? With this object before me,
I might feel a right to live! Without it, it is
a shame for me to have lived so long?

"I fully agree with you," said Kenyon, "that
your true place is by his side."

"Surely it is," replied Miriam. "If Dona-
tello is entitled to aught on earth, it is to my
complete self-sacrifice for his sake. It does not
weaken his claim, methinks, that my only prospect
of happiness—a fearful word, however—lies in
the good that may accrue to him from our inter-
course. But he rejects me! He will not listen
to the whisper of his heart, telling him that she,
most wretched, who beguiled him into evil, might
guide him to a higher innocence than that from
which he fell. How is this first, great difficulty
to be obviated?"

"It lies at your own option, Miriam, to do

away the obstacle, at any moment," remarked
the sculptor. "It is but to ascend Donatello's
tower, and you will meet him there, under the
eye of God."

"I dare not," answered Miriam. "No; I dare
not!"

"Do you fear," asked the sculptor, "the dread
eye-witness whom I have named?"

"No; for, as far as I can see into that cloudy
and inscrutable thing, my heart, it has none but
pure motives," replied Miriam. "But, my friend,
you little know what a weak, or what a strong

seemed the plaything of a moment. But, in
Miriam's eyes, Donatello was always, thenceforth,
invested with the tragic dignity of their hour
of crime ; and, furthermore, the keen and deep
insight, with which her love endowed her, enabled
her to know him far better than he could be
known by ordinary observation. Beyond all
question, since she loved him so, there was a force
in Donatello worthy of her respect and love.

"You see my weakness," said Miriam, flinging
out her hands, as a person does when a defect
is acknowledged, and beyond remedy. "What
I need, now, is an opportunity to show my
strength."

"It has occurred to me," Kenyon remarked,
"that the time is come, when it may be desirable
to remove Donatello from the complete seclusion
in which he buries himself. He has struggled
long enough with one idea. He now needs a
variety of thought, which cannot be otherwise
so readily supplied to him, as through the medium
of a variety of scenes. His mind is awakened

now; his heart, though full of pain, is no longer benumbed. They should have food and solace. If he linger here much longer, I fear that he may sink back into a lethargy. The extreme excitability, which circumstances have imparted to his moral system, has its dangers and its advantages; it being one of the dangers, that an obdurate scar may supervene upon its very tenderness. Solitude has done what it could for him; now, for a while, let him be enticed into the outer world."

"What is your plan, then?" asked Miriam.

"Simply," replied Kenyon, "to persuade Donatello to be my companion in a ramble among these hills and valleys. The little adventures and vicissitudes of travel will do him infinite good. After his recent profound experience, he will re-create the world by the new eyes with which he will regard it. He will escape, I hope, out of a morbid life, and find his way into a healthy one."

"And what is to be my part in this process?"

inquired Miriam, sadly, and not without jealousy.
"You are taking him from me, and putting your-
self, and all manner of living interests, into the
place which I ought to fill!"

"It would rejoice me, Miriam, to yield the
entire responsibility of this office to yourself,"
answered the sculptor. "I do not pretend to
be the guide and counsellor whom Donatello
needs; for, to mention no other obstacle, I am
a man, and between man and man there is always
an insuperable gulf. They can never quite
grasp each other's hands; and therefore man
never derives any intimate help, any heart suste-
nance, from his brother man, but from woman—
his mother, his sister, or his wife. . Be Donatello's
friend at need, therefore, and most gladly will I
resign him!"

"It is not kind to taunt me thus," said
Miriam. "I have told you that I cannot do
what you suggest, because I dare not."

"Well, then," rejoined the sculptor, "see if
there is any possibility of adapting yourself to

my scheme. The incidents of a journey often
fling people together in the oddest, and therefore
the most natural way. Supposing you were to
find yourself on the same route, a reunion with
Donatello might ensue, and Providence have a
larger hand in it than either of us."

"It is not a hopeful plan," said Miriam,
shaking her head, after a moment's thought
"yet I will not reject it without a trial. Only,
in case it fail, here is a resolution to which I
bind myself, come what come may! You know
the bronze statue of Pope Julius in the great
square of Perugia? I remember standing in the
shadow of that statue one sunny noontime and
being impressed by its paternal aspect, and fancy-
ing that a blessing fell upon me from its out-
stretched hand. Ever since, I have had a super-
stition—you will call it foolish, but sad and
ill-fated persons always dream such things—that,
if I waited long enough in that same spot, some
good event would come to pass. Well, my friend,
precisely a fortnight after you begin your tour

unless we sooner meet⊜bring Donatello, at noon, to the base of the statue. You will find me there!"

Kenyon assented to the proposed arrangement, and, after some conversation respecting his contemplated line of travel, prepared to take his leave. As he met Miriam's eyes, in bidding farewell, he was surprised at the new, tender gladness that beamed out of them, and at the appearance of health and bloom, which, in this little while, had overspread her face.

"May I tell you, Miriam," said he, smiling, "that you are still as beautiful as ever?"

"You have a right to notice it," she replied, "for, if it be so, my faded bloom has been revived by the hopes you give me.. Do you, then, think me beautiful? I rejoice, most truly. Beauty—if I possess it—shall be one of the instruments by which I will try to educate and elevate him, to whose good I solely dedicate myself."

The sculptor had nearly reached the door,

when, hearing her call him, he turned back, and
beheld Miriam still standing where he had left
her, in the magnificent hall which seemed only
a fit setting for her beauty. She beckoned him
to return.

"You are a man of refined taste," said she;
"more than that—a man of delicate sensibility.
Now tell me frankly, and on your honour,
have I not shocked you many times during this
interview by my betrayal of woman's cause, my
lack of feminine modesty, my reckless, passionate,
most indecorous avowal, that I live only in the
life of one who perhaps scorns and shudders
at me?"

Thus adjured, however difficult the point
to which she brought him, the sculptor was
not a man to swerve aside from the simple
truth.

"Miriam," replied he, "you exaggerate the

"I knew it," said Miriam, mournfully, *but*
with no resentment. "What remains of my
finer nature would have told me so, even if it
had not been perceptible in all your manner.
Well, my dear friend, when you go back to
Rome, tell Hilda what her severity has done!
She was all Womanhood to me; and when she
cast me off, I had no longer any terms to keep
with the reserves and decorums of my sex.
Hilda has set me free! Pray tell her so, from
Miriam, and thank her!"

"I shall tell Hilda nothing that will give her
pain," answered Kenyon. "But, Miriam, though
I know not what passed between her and your-
self, I feel—and let the noble frankness of your
disposition forgive me, if I say so—I feel that
she was right. You have a thousand admirable
qualities. Whatever mass of evil may have fallen
into your life, pardon me, but your own words
suggest it, you are still as capable as ever of
many high and heroic virtues. But the white
shining purity of Hilda's nature is a thing apart;

and she is bound by the undefiled material of
which God moulded her, to keep that severity
which I, as well as you, have recognized."

" Oh, you are right!" said Miriam; " I never
questioned it; though, as I told you, when she
cast me off, it severed some few remaining bonds
between me and decorous womanhood. But were
there anything to forgive I do forgive her. May
you win her virgin heart; for methinks there
can be few men in this evil world who are not
more unworthy of her than yourself."

· CHAPTER XVI.

SCENES BY THE WAY.

WHEN it came to the point of quitting the re-
poseful life of Monte Beni, the sculptor was
not without regrets, and would willingly have
dreamed a little longer of the sweet paradise on
earth that Hilda's presence there might make.
Nevertheless, amid all its repose, he had begun
to be sensible of a restless melancholy, to which
the cultivators of the ideal arts are more liable
than sturdier men. On his own part, therefore,
and leaving Donatello out of the case, he would
have judged it well to go. He made parting
visits to the legendary dell, and to other de-
lightful spots with which he had grown familiar;
he climbed the tower again, and saw a sunset
and a moonrise over the great valley; he drank,

on the eve of his departure, one flask, and then
another, of the Monte Beni Sunshine, and stored
up its flavour in his memory, as the standard
of what is exquisite in wine. These things ac-
complished, Kenyon was ready for the journey.

Donatello had not very easily been stirred
out of the peculiar sluggishness, which enthrals
and bewitches melancholy people. He had of-
fered merely a passive resistance, however, not
an active one, to his friend's schemes; and
when the appointed hour came, he yielded to
the impulse which Kenyon failed not to apply;
and was started upon the journey before he had
made up his mind to undertake it. They
wandered forth at large, like two knights-errant,
among the valleys, and the mountains, and the
old mountain-towns of that picturesque and
lovely region. Save to keep the appointment
with Miriam, a fortnight thereafter, in the great
square of Perugia, there was nothing more de-
finite in the sculptor's plan than that they
should let themselves be blown hither and thither

like winged seeds, that mount upon each wander-
ing breeze. Yet there was an idea of fatality
implied in the simile of the winged seeds, which
did not altogether suit Kenyon's fancy; for,
if you look closely into the matter, it will be
seen that whatever appears most vagrant, and
utterly purposeless, turns out, in the end, to
have been impelled the most surely on a pre-
ordained and unswerving track. Chance and
change love to deal with men's settled plans,
not with their idle vagaries. If we desire un-
expected and unimaginable events, we should
contrive an iron framework, such as we fancy
may compel the future to take one inevitable
shape ; then comes in the Unexpected, and
shatters our design in fragments.

The travellers set forth on horseback, and
purposed to perform much of their aimless jour-
neyings, under the moon, and in the cool of
the morning or evening twilight ; the mid-day sun,
while summer had hardly begun to trail its

departing skirts over Tuscany, being still too
fervid to allow of noontide exposure.

For a while, they wandered in that same broad
valley which Kenyon had viewed with such
delight from the Monte Beni tower. The sculptor
soon began to enjoy the idle activity of their new
life, which the lapse of a day or two sufficed
to establish as a kind of system; it is so natural
for mankind to be nomadic, that a very little taste
of that primitive mode of existence subverts the
settled habits of many preceding years. Ken-
yon's cares, and whatever gloomy ideas before
possessed him, seemed to be left at Monte Beni,
and were scarcely remembered by the time that
its gray tower grew undistinguishable on the
brown hill-side. His perceptive faculties which
had found little exercise of late, amid so thought-
ful a way of life, became keen, and kept his
eyes busy with a hundred agreeable scenes.

He delighted in the picturesque bits of rustic
character and manners, so little of which ever

comes upon the surface of our life at home.
There, for example, were the old women, tending
pigs or sheep by the wayside. As they followed
the vagrant steps of their charge, these vene-
rable ladies kept spinning yarn with that else-
where forgotten contrivance, the distaff; and so
wrinkled and stern-looking were they, that you
might have taken them for the Parcæ, spinning
the threads of human destiny. In contrast
with their great-grandmothers were the children,
leading goats of shaggy beard, tied by the horns,
and letting them browze on branch and shrub.
It is the fashion of Italy to add the petty industry
of age and childhood to the sum of human toil.
To the eyes of an observer from the western
world, it was a strange spectacle to see sturdy,
sunburnt creatures, in petticoats, but otherwise
manlike, toiling side by side with male labourers,
in the rudest work of the fields. These sturdy
women (if as such we must recognize them)
wore the high-crowned, broad-brimmed hat of
Tuscan straw, the customary female head-apparel;

and, as every breeze blew back its breadth of brim, the sunshine constantly added depth to the brown glow of their cheeks. The elder sisterhood, however, set off their witch-like ugliness to the worst advantage with black felt hats, bequeathed them, one would fancy, by their long-buried husbands.

Another ordinary sight, as sylvan as the above, and more agreeable, was a girl, bearing on her back a huge bundle of green twigs and shrubs, or grass, intermixed with scarlet poppies and blue flowers; the verdant burden being sometimes of such size as to hide the bearer's figure, and seem a self-moving mass of fragrant bloom and verdure. Oftener, however, the bundle reached only half-way down the back of the rustic nymph, leaving in sight her well-developed lower limbs, and the crooked knife, hanging behind her, with which she had been reaping this strange harvest sheaf. A pre-Raphaelite artist (he, for instance, who painted so marvel-

might find an admirable subject in one of these
Tuscan girls, stepping with a free, erect, and
graceful carriage. The miscellaneous herbage and
tangled twigs and blossoms of her bundle, crowning
her head (while her ruddy, comely face looks out
between the hanging side festoons like a larger
flower) would give the painter boundless scope for
the minute delineation which he loves.

Though mixed up with what was rude and
earthlike, there was still a remote, dreamlike,
Arcadian charm, which is scarcely to be found
in the daily toil of other lands. Among the
pleasant features of the wayside were always
the vines, clambering on fig-trees, or other
sturdy trunks; they wreathed themselves, in
huge and rich festoons, from one tree to another,
suspending clusters of ripening grapes in the
interval between. Under such careless mode of
culture, the luxuriant vine is a lovelier spectacle
than where it produces a more precious liquor,
and is therefore more artificially restrained and
trimmed. Nothing can be more picturesque than

an old grape-vine, with almost a trunk of its own, clinging fast around its supporting tree. Nor does the picture lack its moral. You might twist it to more than one grave purpose, as you saw how the knotted, serpentine growth imprisoned within its strong embrace the friend that had supported its tender infancy; and how (as seemingly flexible natures are prone to do) it converted the sturdier tree entirely to its own selfish ends, extending its innumerable arms on every bough, and permitting hardly a leaf to sprout except its own. It occurred to Kenyon, that the enemies of the vine, in his native land, might here have seen an emblem of the remorseless gripe which the habit of vinous enjoyment lays upon its victim, possessing him wholly, and letting him live no life but such as it bestows.

The scene was not less characteristic when their path led the two wanderers through some small ancient town. There, besides the peculiarities of present life, they saw tokens of the life that had long ago been lived and flung aside. The little

town, such as we see in our mind's eye, would
have its gate and its surrounding walls, so ancient
and massive that ages had not sufficed to crumble
them away; but in the lofty upper portion of
the gateway, still standing over the empty arch,
where there was no longer a gate to shut, there
would be a dovecote, and peaceful doves for
the only warders. Pumpkins lay ripening in
the open chambers of the structure. Then, as
for the town-wall, on the outside an orchard ex-
tends peacefully along its base, full, not of apple-
trees, but of those old humorists with gnarled
trunks and twisted boughs, the olives. Houses
have been built upon the ramparts, or burrowed
out of their ponderous foundation. Even the
gray, martial towers crowned with ruined turrets,
have been converted into rustic habitations, from
the windows of which hang ears of Indian corn.

whole line of ancient wall, so that it seems a
row of dwellings with one continuous front, built
in a strange style of needless strength; but
remnants of the old battlements and machicola-
tions are interspersed with the homely chambers
and earthen-tiled house-tops; and all along its
extent both grape-vines and running flower-shrubs
are encouraged to clamber and sport over the
roughnesses of its decay.

Finally, the long grass, intermixed with weeds
and wild-flowers, waves on the uppermost height
of the shattered rampart; and it is exceedingly

Passing through the gateway of this same little
town, challenged only by those watchful sentinels,
the pigeons, we find ourselves in a long narrow
street, paved from side to side with flag-stones,
in the old Roman fashion. Nothing can exceed
the grim ugliness of the houses, most of which
are three or four stories high, stone-built, gray,
dilapidated, or half covered with plaster in patches,
and contiguous all along from end to end of the
town. Nature, in the shape of tree, shrub, or
grassy side-walk, is as much shut out from the
one street of the rustic village as from the heart
of any swarming city. The dark and half-ruinous
habitations, with their small windows, many of
which are drearily closed with wooden shutters,
are but magnified hovels, piled story upon story,
and squalid with the grime that successive ages
have left behind them. It would be a hideous
scene to contemplate in a rainy day, or when
no human life pervaded it. In the summer-noon,
however, it possesses vivacity enough to keep
itself cheerful; for all the within-doors of the

village then bubbles over upon the flag-stones, or looks out from the small windows, and from here and there a balcony. Some of the populace are at the butcher's shop; others are at the fountain, which gushes into a marble basin that resembles an antique sarcophagus. A tailor is sewing before his door, with a young priest seated sociably beside him; a burly friar goes by with an empty wine-barrel on his head; children are at play; women at their own doorsteps mend clothes, embroider, weave hats of Tuscan straw, or twirl the distaff. Many idlers, meanwhile, strolling from one group to another, let the warm day slide by in the sweet, interminable task of doing nothing.

From all these people there comes a babblement that seems quite disproportioned to the number of tongues that make it. So many words are not uttered in a New England village throughout the year, except it be at a political caucus or town-meeting, as are spoken here, with no especial purpose, in a single day. Neither

so many words, nor so much laughter; for
people talk about nothing as if they were ter-
ribly in earnest, and make merry at nothing,
as if it were the best of all possible jokes. In
so long a time as they have existed, and with-
in such narrow precincts, these little walled
towns are brought into a closeness of society
that makes them but a larger household. All
the inhabitants are akin to each, and each to
all; they assemble in the street as their com-
mon saloon, and thus live and die in a fami-
liarity of intercourse, such as never can be
known where a village is open at either end,
and all roundabout, and has ample room with-
in itself.

Stuck up beside the door of one house, in
this village street, is a withered bough; and,
on a stone seat, just under the shadow of the
bough, sits a party of jolly drinkers, making
proof of the new wine, or quaffing the old,
as their often-tried and comfortable friend. Ken-
yon draws bridle here (for the bough; or bush,

be welcome now. Meanwhile, Donatello has
ridden onward, but alights where a shrine, with
a burning lamp before it, is built into the wall
of an inn-stable. He kneels, and crosses him-
self, and mutters a brief prayer, without attract-
ing notice from the passers-by; many of whom
are parenthetically devout, in a similar fashion.
By this time the sculptor has drunk off his
wine-and-water, and our two travellers resume
their way, emerging from the opposite gate of
the village.

Before them, again, lies the broad valley,
with a mist so thinly scattered over it as to be
perceptible only in the distance, and most so
in the nooks of the hills. Now that we have
called it mist, it seems a mistake not rather to
have called it sunshine; the glory of so much

light being mingled with so little gloom, in
the airy material of that vapour. Be it mist
or sunshine, it adds a touch of ideal beauty to
the scene, almost persuading the spectator that
this valley and those hills are visionary, be-
cause their visible atmosphere is so like the
substance of a dream.

Immediately about them, however, there were
abundant tokens that the country was not really
the paradise it looked to be, at a casual glance.
Neither the wretched cottages nor the dreary
farmhouses seemed to partake of the prosperity,
with which so kindly a climate, and so fertile
a portion of Mother Earth's bosom, should have
filled them, one and all. But, possibly, the
peasant inhabitants do not exist in so grimy a
poverty, and in homes so comfortless, as a
stranger, with his native ideas of those matters,
would be likely to imagine. The Italians ap-
pear ·to possess none of that emulative pride
which we see in our New England villages,
where every householder, according to his taste

and means, endeavours to make his homestead an ornament to the grassy and elm-shadowed wayside. In Italy there are no neat doorsteps and thresholds; no pleasant, vine-sheltered porches; none of those grass-plots or smoothly shorn lawns, which hospitably invite the imagination into the sweet domestic interiors of English life. Everything, however sunny and luxuriant may be the scene around, is especially disheartening in the immediate neighbourhood of an Italian home.

An artist, it is true, might often thank his stars for those old houses, so picturesquely time-stained, and with the plaster falling in blotches from the ancient brickwork. The prison-like, iron-barred windows, and the wide-arched, dismal entrance, admitting on one hand to the stable, on the other to the kitchen, might impress him as far better worth his pencil than the newly painted pine boxes, in which if he be an American his countrymen live and thrive. But there is reason to suspect that a people are waning to decay and ruin the moment that their life becomes fascinating either in the poet's imagination or the painter's eye.

As usual on Italian waysides, the wanderers passed great black crosses, hung with all the instruments of the sacred agony and passion; there were the crown of thorns, the hammer and nails, the pincers, the spear, the sponge, and perched over the whole, the cock that crowed to Saint Peter's remorseful conscience. Thus, while the fertile scene showed the never-failing beneficence of the Creator towards man in his transitory state, these symbols reminded each wayfarer of the Saviour's infinitely greater love for him as an immortal spirit. Beholding these consecrated stations, the idea seemed to strike Donatello of converting the otherwise aimless journey into a penitential pilgrimage. At each of them he alighted to kneel and kiss the cross, and humbly press his forehead against its foot; and this so invariably, that the sculptor soon learned to draw bridle of his own accord. It may be, too, conscience, and the pardon of the sin that so oppressed him.

Not only at the crosses did Donatello kneel, but at each of the many shrines, where the blessed Virgin in fresco faded with sunshine and half washed out with showers looked benignly at her worshipper; or where she was represented in a wooden image, or a bas-relief of plaster or marble, as accorded with the means of the devout person who built, or restored from a mediæval antiquity, these places of wayside worship. They were everywhere; under arched niches, or in little pent-houses with a brick tiled roof, just large enough to shelter them; or perhaps in some bit of old Roman masonry, the founders of which had died before the Advent; or in the wall of a country inn or farmhouse, or at the midway point of a bridge, or in the shallow cavity of a natural rock, or of judgment.

It was beautiful to observe, indeed, how tender was the soul of man and woman towards the Virgin mother, in recognition of the tenderness which, as their faith taught them, she immortally cherishes towards all human souls. In the wire-work screen, before each shrine, hung offerings of roses, or whatever flower was sweetest and most seasonable; some already wilted and withered, some fresh with that very morning's dewdrops. Flowers there were, too, that, being artificial, never bloomed on earth, nor would ever fade. The thought occurred to Kenyon, that flower-pots with living plants might be set within the niches, or even that rose-trees, and all kinds of flowering shrubs, might be reared under the shrines and taught to twine and wreath themselves around; so that the Virgin should dwell within a bower of verdure, bloom, and fragrant freshness, symbolizing a homage perpetually new. There are many things in the religious customs of these people that seem good; many things, at least, that might be both good and beautiful, if the soul of goodness and the sense of beauty were as much alive in the Italians now, as they must have been when those customs were first imagined and adopted. But, instead of blossoms on the shrub, or freshly gathered, with the dewdrops on their leaves, their worship, now-a-days, is best symbolized by the artificial flower.

The sculptor fancied, moreover (but perhaps it was his heresy that suggested the idea), that it would be of happy influence to place a comfortable and shady seat beneath every wayside shrine. Then, the weary and sun-scorched traveller, while resting himself under her protecting shadow, might thank the Virgin for her hos-

pitality. Nor, perchance, were he to regale him-
self, even in such a consecrated spot, with the
fragrance of a pipe, would it rise to heaven more
offensively than the smoke of priestly incense.
We do ourselves wrong, and too meanly estimate
the Holiness above us, when we deem that any
act or enjoyment, good in itself, is not good to
do religiously.

Whatever may be the iniquities of the papal
system, it was a wise and lovely sentiment, that
set up the frequent shrine and cross along the
roadside. No wayfarer, bent on whatever worldly
errand, can fail to be reminded, at every mile
or two, that this is not the business which most
concerns him. The pleasure-seeker is silently
admonished to look heavenward for a joy in-
finitely greater than he now possesses. The
wretch in temptation beholds the cross, and is
warned, that if he yield, the Saviour's agony for
his sake will have been endured in vain. The
stubborn criminal, whose heart has long been
like a stone, feels it throb anew with dread and

helped him towards a higher penitence.

Whether the young Count of Monte Beni noticed the fact, or no, there was more than one incident of their journey that led Kenyon to believe, that they were attended, or closely followed, or preceded, near at hand, by some one who took an interest in their motions. As it were, the step, the sweeping garment, the faintly-heard breath, of an invisible companion, was beside them, as they went on their way. It was like a dream that had strayed out of their slumber and was haunting them in the daytime, when its shadowy substance could have neither density nor outline, in the too obtrusive light. After sunset, it grew a little more distinct.

"On the left of that last shrine," asked the sculptor, as they rode, under the moon, "did you observe the figure of a woman kneeling, with her face hidden in her hands?"

"I never looked that way," replied Donatello. "I was saying my own prayer. It was some penitent, perchance. May the Blessed Virgin be the more gracious to the poor soul, because she is a woman."

CHAPTER XVII.

PICTURED WINDOWS.

AFTER wide wanderings through the valley, the two travellers directed their course towards its boundary of hills. Here, the natural scenery and men's modifications of it immediately took a different aspect from that of the fertile and smiling plain. Not unfrequently there was a convent on the hillside; or, on some insulated promontory, a ruined castle, once the den of a robber chieftain, who was accustomed to dash down from his commanding height upon the road that wound below. For ages back, the old fortress had been flinging down its crumbling ramparts, stone by stone, towards the grimy village at its foot.

Their road wound onward among the hills,

which rose steep and lofty from the scanty level space that lay between them. They continually thrust their great bulks before the wayfarers, as if grimly resolute to forbid their passage, or closed abruptly behind them, when they still dared to proceed. A gigantic hill would set its foot right down before them, and only at the last moment would grudgingly withdraw it, just far enough to let them creep towards another obstacle. Adown these rough heights were visible the dry tracks of many a mountain-torrent, that had lived a life too fierce and passionate to be a long one. Or, perhaps a stream was yet hurrying shyly along the edge of a far wider bed of pebbles and shelving rock than it seemed to need, though not too wide for the swollen rage of which this shy rivulet was capable. A stone bridge bestrode it, the ponderous arches of which were upheld and rendered indestructible by the weight of the very stones that threatened to crush them down. Old Roman toil was perceptible in the foundations of that

massive bridge; the first weight that it ever
bore was that of an army of the Republic. &c

Threading these defiles, they would arrive at
some immemorial city, crowning the high summit
of a hill with its cathedral, its many churches,
and public edifices, all of Gothic architecture.
With no more level ground than a single piazza,
in the midst, the ancient town tumbled its crooked
and narrow streets down the mountain side,
through arched passages and by steps of stone.
The aspect of everything was awfully old; older,
indeed, in its effect on the imagination, than Rome
itself, because history does not lay its finger on
these forgotten edifices and tell us all about their
origin. Etruscan princes may have dwelt in
them. A thousand years, at all events, would
seem but a middle age for these structures.
They are built of such huge, square stones, that
their appearance of ponderous durability distresses
the beholder with the idea that they can never
fall—never crumble away—never be less fit than
now for human habitation. Many of them may

once have been palaces, and still retain a squalid
grandeur. But, gazing at them, we recognize
how undesirable it is to build the tabernacle of
our brief lifetime out of permanent materials, and
with a view to their being occupied by future
generations.

All towns should be made capable of purifi-
cation by fire, or of decay within each half-
century. Otherwise, they become the hereditary
haunts of vermin and noisomeness, besides stand-
ing apart from the possibility of such improve-
ments as are constantly introduced into the rest
of man's contrivances and accommodations. It
is beautiful, no doubt, and exceedingly satisfactory
to some of our natural instincts, to imagine our
far posterity dwelling under the same roof-tree
as ourselves. Still, when people insist on building
indestructible houses, they incur, or their children
do, a misfortune analogous to that of the Sibyl,
when she obtained the grievous boon of immor-
tality. So, we may build almost immortal habi-
tations, it is true; but we cannot keep them from

growing old, musty, unwholesome, dreary, full of death-scents, ghosts, and murder-stains; in short, habitations such as one sees everywhere in Italy, be they hovels or palaces.

"You should go with me to my native country," observed the sculptor to Donatello. "In that fortunate land, each generation has only its own sins and sorrows to bear. Here, it seems as if all the weary and dreary Past were piled upon the back of the Present. If I were to lose my spirits in this country—if I were to suffer any heavy misfortune here—methinks it would be impossible to stand up against it, under such adverse influences."

"The sky itself is an old roof, now," answered the count; "and, no doubt, the sins of mankind have made it gloomier than it used to be."

"Oh, my poor Faun," thought Kenyon to himself, "how art thou changed !"

A city, like this of which we speak, seems a sort of stony growth out of the hill-side, or a

fossilized town; so ancient and strange it looks,
without enough of life and juiciness in it to be
any longer susceptible of decay. An earthquake
would afford it the only chance of being ruined,
beyond its present ruin.

Yet, though dead to all the purposes for which
we live to-day, the place has its glorious recollec-
tions, and not merely rude and warlike ones,
but those of brighter and milder triumphs, the
fruits of which we still enjoy. Italy can count
several of these lifeless towns which, four or
five hundred years ago, were each the birth-
place of its own school of art; nor have they
yet forgotten to be proud of the dark, old pic-
tures, and the faded frescoes, the pristine beauty
of which was a light and gladness to the world.
But now, unless one happens to be a painter,
these famous works make us miserably desperate.
They are poor, dim ghosts of what, when Giotto
or Cimabue first created them, threw a splendour
along the stately aisles; so far gone towards
nothingness, in our day, that scarcely a hint of

design or expression can glimmer through the dusk. Those early artists did well to paint their frescoes. Glowing on the church walls, they might be looked upon as symbols of the living spirit that made Catholicism a true religion, and that glorified it as long as it retained a genuine life; they filled the transepts with a radiant throng of saints and angels, and threw around the high altar a faint reflection—as much as mortals could see, or bear—of a Diviner Presence. But, now that the colours are so wretchedly bedimmed—now that blotches of plastered wall dot the frescoes all over, like a mean reality thrusting itself through life's brightest illusions—the next best artist to Cimabue, or Giotto, or Ghirlandaio, or Pinturicchio, will be he that shall reverently cover their ruined masterpieces with whitewash!

Kenyon, however, being an earnest student and critic of Art, lingered long before these pathetic relics; and Donatello, in his present phase of penitence, thought no time spent amiss

while he could be kneeling before an altar.
Whenever they found a cathedral, therefore, or
a Gothic church, the two travellers were of one
mind to enter it. In some of these holy edifices
they saw pictures that time had not dimmed nor
injured in the least, though they perhaps belonged
to as old a school of Art as any that were perish-
ing around them. These were the painted win-
dows; and as often as he gazed at them, the
sculptor blessed the mediæval time, and its gor-
geous contrivances of splendour; for surely the
skill of man has never accomplished, nor his
mind imagined, any other beauty or glory worthy
to be compared with these.

It is the special excellence of pictured glass,
that the light, which falls merely on the outside
of other pictures, is here interfused throughout
the work; it illuminates the design, and invests
it with a living radiance; and in requital, the
unfading colours transmute the common daylight
into a miracle of richness and glory in its passage
through the heavenly substance of the blessed

and angelic shapes which throng the high-arched
window.

"It is a woeful thing," cried Kenyon, while
one of these frail, yet enduring and fadeless
pictures threw its hues on his face, and on the
pavement of the church around him,—"a sad
necessity that any Christian soul should pass from
earth without once seeing an antique painted
window, with the bright Italian sunshine glowing
through it! There is no other such true symbol
of the glories of the better world, where a celestial
radiance will be inherent in all things and persons,
and render each continually transparent to the
sight of all."

"But what a horror it would be," said Dona-
tello, sadly, "if there were a soul among them
through which the light could not be trans-
fused."

"Yes; and perhaps this is to be the punish-
ment of sin," replied the sculptor; "not that it
shall be made evident to the universe, which
can profit nothing by such knowledge, but that

it shall insulate the sinner from all sweet society
by rendering him impermeable to light, and
therefore, unrecognizable in the abode of heavenly
simplicity and truth. Then, what remains for
him, but the dreariness of infinite and eternal
solitude."

"That would be a horrible destiny, indeed!"
said Donatello.

His voice, as he spoke the words, had a hollow
and dreary cadence, as if he anticipated some
such frozen solitude for himself. A figure in a
dark robe was lurking in the obscurity of a side-
chapel close by, and made an impulsive move-
ment forward, but hesitated as Donatello spoke
again.

"But there might be a more miserable torture
than to be solitary for ever," said he. "Think
of having a single companion in eternity, and
instead of finding any consolation, or at all events
variety of torture, to see your own weary, weary
sin repeated in that inseparable soul?"

"I think, my dear count, you have never

read Dante," observed Kenyon. "That idea is somewhat in his style, but I cannot help regretting that it came into your mind just then."

The dark-robed figure had shrunk back, and was quite lost to sight among the shadows of the chapel.

"There was an English poet," resumed Kenyon, turning again towards the window, "who speaks of the 'dim, religious light,' transmitted through painted glass. I always admired this richly descriptive phrase; but, though he was once in Italy, I question whether Milton ever saw any but the dingy pictures in the dusty windows of English cathedrals, imperfectly shown by the gray English daylight. He would else have illuminated that word, 'dim,' with some epithet that should not chase away the dimness, yet should make it glow like a million of rubies, sapphires, emeralds, and topazes. Is it not so with yonder window? The pictures are most brilliant in themselves, yet dim with tenderness and reverence, because God himself is shining through them.

"The pictures fill me with emotion, but not such as you seem to experience," said Donatello. "I tremble at those awful saints; and, most of all, at the figure above them. He glows with Divine wrath!"

"My dear friend," exclaimed Kenyon, "how strangely your eyes have transmuted the expression of the figure! It is divine love, not wrath."

"To my eyes," said Donatello stubbornly, "it is wrath, not love! Each must interpret for himself."

The friends left the church, and, looking up from the exterior, at the window which they had just been contemplating within, nothing was visible but the merest outline of dusky shapes. Neither the individual likeness of saint, angel, nor Saviour, and far less the combined scheme and purport of the picture, could anywise be made out. That miracle of radiant art, thus viewed, was nothing better than an incompre-

hensible obscurity, without a gleam of beauty
to induce the beholder to attempt unravelling it.
"All this," thought the sculptor, "is a most
forcible emblem of the different aspect of reli-
gious truth and sacred story, as viewed from the
warm interior of belief, or from its cold and
dreary outside. Christian faith is a grand ca-
thedral, with divinely pictured windows. Stand-
ing without, you see no glory, nor can possibly
imagine any; standing within, every ray of
light reveals a harmony of unspeakable splen-
dours."

After Kenyon and Donatello emerged from
the church, however, they had better opportunity
for acts of charity and mercy than for religious
contemplation; being immediately surrounded by
a swarm of beggars, who are the present pos-
sessors of Italy, and share the spoil of the
stranger with the fleas and mosquitoes, their for-
midable allies. These pests—the human ones
—had hunted the two travellers at every
stage of their journey. From village to village

ragged boys and girls kept almost under
the horses' feet; hoary grandsires and grand-
dames caught glimpses of their approach, and
hobbled to intercept them at some point of
vantage; blind men stared them out of coun-
tenance with their sightless orbs; women held
up their unwashed babies; cripples displayed
their wooden legs, their grievous scars, their
dangling, boneless arms, their broken backs,
their burden of a hump, or whatever infirmity
or deformity Providence had assigned them for
an inheritance. On the highest mountain summit
—in the most shadowy ravine—there was a
beggar waiting for them. In one small village,
Kenyon had the curiosity to count merely how
many children were crying, whining, and bellow-
ing all at once for alms. They proved to be
more than forty of as ragged and dirty little
imps as any in the world; besides whom all the
wrinkled matrons, and most of the village maids,
and not a few stalwart men, held out their hands
grimly, piteously, or smilingly, in the forlorn

37—2

hope of whatever trifle of coin might remain in
pockets already so fearfully taxed. Had they
been permitted, they would gladly have knelt
down and worshipped the travellers, and have
cursed them, without rising from their knees, if
the expected boon failed to be awarded.

Yet they were not so miserably poor but that
the grown people kept houses over their heads.
In the way of food, they had, at least, vegetables
in their little gardens, pigs and chickens to kill,
eggs to fry into omelets with oil, wine to drink,
and many other things to make life comfortable.
As for the children, when no more small coin
appeared to be forthcoming, they began to laugh
and play, and turn heels over head, showing
themselves jolly and vivacious brats, and evi-
dently as well fed as need be. The truth is,
the Italian peasantry look upon strangers as the
almoners of Providence, and therefore feel no
more shame in asking and receiving alms, than
in availing themselves of providential bounties in
whatever other form.

In accordance with his nature, Donatello was always exceedingly charitable to these ragged battalions, and appeared to derive a certain consolation from the prayers which many of them put up in his behalf. In Italy a copper coin of minute value will often make all the difference between a vindictive curse—death by apoplexy being the favourite one—mumbled in an old witch's toothless jaws, and a prayer from the same lips, so earnest that it would seem to reward the charitable soul with at least a puff of grateful breath to help him heavenward. Good wishes being so cheap, though possibly not very efficacious, and anathemas so exceedingly bitter—even if the greater portion of their poison remain in the mouth that utters them—it may be wise to expend some reasonable amount in the purchase of the former. Donatello invariably did so; and as he distributed his alms under the pictured window, of which we have been speaking, no less than seven ancient women lifted their hands and besought blessings on his head.

"Come," said the sculptor, rejoicing at the happier expression which he saw in his friend's face, "I think your steed will not stumble with you to-day. Each of these old dames looks as much like Horace's Atra Cura as can well be conceived; but, though there are seven of them, they will make your burden on horseback lighter, instead of heavier."

"Are we to ride far?" asked the count.

"A tolerable journey betwixt now and to-morrow noon," Kenyon replied; "for, at that hour, I purpose to be standing by the Pope's statue in the great square of Perugia."